If . . . Then . . . Curriculum: Assessment-Based Instruction, Grade 5

Lucy Calkins with Colleagues from the Teachers College Reading and Writing Project

Photography by Peter Cunningham

HEINEMANN ◆ PORTSMOUTH, NH

*first*hand
An imprint of Heinemann
361 Hanover Street
Portsmouth, NH 03801–3912
www.heinemann.com

Offices and agents throughout the world

Cataloging-in-Publication data is on file with the Library of Congress.

ISBN-13: 978-0-325-04815-4
ISBN-10: 0-325-04815-0

Production: Elizabeth Valway, David Stirling, and Abigail Heim
Cover and interior designs: Jenny Jensen Greenleaf
Series includes photographs by Peter Cunningham, Nadine Baldasare, and Elizabeth Dunford
Composition: Publishers' Design and Production Services, Inc.
Manufacturing: Steve Bernier

Printed in the United States of America on acid-free paper
17 16 15 14 13 ML 1 2 3 4 5

Contents

PART TWO: Differentiating Instruction for Individuals and Small Groups: If . . . Then . . . Conferring Scenarios

Introduction

THIS BOOK IS WRITTEN to help fifth-grade teachers whose students enter their classroom already able to fashion a shapely essay, to use evidence to support claims, to synthesize information into a series of chapters—the works. It is also written to help teachers whose students respond to the invitation to write by asking, "How long does it have to be?" and by saying, "I can't think of anything to write about." The spread becomes bigger each year as students who have had a background in writing become progressively more skilled, and those who have not been taught writing at all become progressively more resistant.

Of course, students will not only enter fifth grade with varied backgrounds in writing. They'll also come with varied backgrounds in reading and in spelling. Just as young people who have strong literacy in their first language can transfer these skills to reading and writing in a second language and make efficient progress, so too, youngsters with strong language skills in reading and spelling can use those skills to make more rapid progress as writers. But if children enter fifth grade with no background in writing and a shaky foundation in reading and spelling, the challenges compound.

The first half of the alternative units in this book are geared more toward teachers whose fifth-graders do not have a strong background in writing, and the second half of the alternative units, toward students who are ready for more, more, more. Of course, ideally, all students are given access to the exciting genres in the second half of this book, since these topics—poetry, journalism, and fantasy—are among students' favorites.

ON-DEMAND ASSESSMENTS WILL HELP YOU PRIORITIZE WRITING INSTRUCTION AND ADJUST YOUR CURRICULUM

So, first things first. You need to do a quick needs assessment. Ask students to complete one of the on-demand writing assessments found in the book *Writing Pathways: Performance Assessments and Learning Progressions, Grades K–5*. Watch them as they write, and within a few minutes, you'll have a strong sense of the challenges you face. If many of your students can't think of something to write about, write in handwriting too small to see, or eke out little more than half a page in 50 minutes of writing time—and especially if they also produce a page that is riddled with errors—you'll know that your students are facing a steep learning curve. If your students are able to write, but their writing seems as if it is more a display of penmanship and spelling than an effort to communicate ideas and information, if the sentences flow along smoothly but don't carry a cargo of specifics, chances are good that those students have the foundational language skills to write fluently but have not received much instruction in qualities of good writing or strategies of writing well. These students, too, will have a steep learning curve.

In both of these instances, the first thing you will need to do is to think seriously about your commitment to teaching writing. Look over your schedule and your priorities, and then consider how much time you can commit to writing instruction. For your students to meet the ambitious standards of the CCSS, you really need to make writing instruction a huge priority and to convey this message to your students. I strongly suggest you make that choice and teach writing with intense commitment, because the truth is that young writers are incredibly vulnerable to instruction. Time and again, I've seen a teacher turn an entire class of students around in "hold your hat" dramatic ways that are immediately obvious to everyone. But this requires a ferocious will, a laser focus, and a firm resolve to say no to other things to make writing a special priority.

Then again, if students come to you as capable writers, you'll see this right away. When producing on-demand writing, these youngsters will draw upon learned strategies. If they are writing narratives, you'll see evidence of direct quotations, leads that begin with action or dialogue, and an appreciation for detail and for structure. In the one fleeting year in front of you, these youngsters are poised to become proficient not just at the fifth-grade CCSS but also at all the sixth-grade and even some of the seventh-grade standards. (The gap between the fifth- and sixth-grade standards is not large, and yet there is a giant leap to be made when moving from the sixth- to the seventh-grade standards. Helping children bridge that gap now will set them on solid ground later on.)

AN OVERVIEW OF THE EXPECTATIONS AND SUPPORTS IN THE FIFTH-GRADE UNITS AND DEVELOPING AN IF . . . THEN . . . CURRICULUM BASED ON YOUR CHILDREN'S NEEDS

The books in the series, Units of Study in Opinion, Information, and Narrative Writing, Fifth Grade, are rigorous. When you assess fifth-graders at the start of the year, remember that if they are perfectly on track, their narratives will for the most part align to the fourth-grade checklist. That checklist reflects what children should be able to do at the end of fourth grade; you are absolutely *not* expecting children to enter fifth grade producing on-demand writing that is at the end-of-fifth-grade level. You should feel very pleased if many of your children are somewhere in the ballpark of writing at the fourth-grade level; this means they haven't had summer slippage and are starting fifth grade just about where they should be.

If your students have not had any writing experience and their writing does not come close to aligning to fifth-grade standards for narrative writing, you'd profit from considering teaching an introductory narrative unit before beginning *Narrative Craft*, and there are a number of paths you might take. First,

if colleagues in your school also have this Units of Study series, you might consider drawing from a unit or two that were designed for earlier grades. This would not be repetitious for your students, because the whole point is that they aren't performing at grade level in writing! You could lean on *The Arc of Story: Writing Realistic Fiction*, both fourth-grade units. If you or your school has copies of the original Units of Study series, you could rely on the first book in that original series: *Launching the Writing Workshop*.

Narrative Craft is written so that students will be successful in *Shaping Texts: From Essay and Narrative to Memoir*. The latter is a challenging text because it supports not only narrative but also essay writing and helps students to draw on all they know about both narrative and opinion writing to shape a text where the structure supports meaning (CCSS 7).

Meanwhile, you also need to think about a progression of work supporting information writing and research, so you will also conduct an information on-demand assessment. *The Lens of History: Research Reports* assumes some background in information writing. This book is an ambitious unit on research-based information writing and is written with the expectation that when asked to produce an on-demand information text, students will categorize information and ideas, writing a text that tackles one subtopic separately from another. It also is assumed that students can link one piece of information together with another or one piece of information with a thought about that information.

Fifth-grade teachers whose students have little or no background in information writing may want to teach a precursor unit prior to *The Lens of History: Research Reports*. We recommend a unit—perhaps a quick one—that aims to teach the strategies and skills of information writing while students write feature articles or nonfiction books on topics of personal expertise. It is far easier to write with information and ideas if one has a command of the facts. Imagine that you were studying a course on nonfiction writing, and the goal was to publish a credible nonfiction text a month from now. Wouldn't you find that challenge vastly easier if the topic could be one that you know well?

In fact, we actually think that even if your students do enter fifth grade with a background in information writing, you might still decide to teach your whole class a quick unit on writing information texts about topics of personal expertise before tackling *The Lens of History*. *The Lens of History* ties into a study of Westward Expansion (though you could alter the topic for your class), so you will ideally want to time your teaching of that unit so that it follows your study of Westward Expansion in social studies.

If you decide to teach a precursor unit on information writing, you have a variety of choices. First, you might decide to draw upon the write-up in this book titled "Information Writing: Feature Articles on Topics of Personal Expertise" to teach your students the basics of information writing as they write about topics they are experts on. Don't let the reference to feature articles dissuade you. This is a basic, meat-and-potatoes unit, masked under the motivating invitation to write feature articles.

You also might consider the second information write-up in this book, "Information Writing: Reading, Research, and Writing in the Content Areas," as a precursor to *The Lens of History*. If you compare and contrast *The Lens of History* and that unit, you'll probably find that they are roughly comparable in challenge level, with *The Lens of History* perhaps being a bit more challenging. But mostly, these simply represent two different takes on a unit on writing research and are both equally applicable to any content area topic. "Writing in the Content Areas" is more traditional, and it will be more familiar to you, which is why it could easily precede *The Lens of History*. Alternatively, you could choose to teach this unit after *The Lens of History*.

The final unit in the fifth-grade series, *The Research-Based Argument Essay*, could actually be taught before or after *The Lens of History*. It assumes a background in essay writing; students who have not grown up within classrooms that teach Units of Study in Writing may have learned essay writing in other ways, which would be fine. The important thing is for writers to enter the unit already able to write a traditional essay in which the writer states a claim and some supporting reasons and then proceeds to develop each of those supporting reasons. If your students do not have any experience writing essays, we've included two units in this book that will help. The first, "The Personal and Persuasive Essay: Boxes and Bullets and Argument Structures for Essay Writing," is designed to help children develop the basic competencies they need when writing well-structured, organized, and cohesive essays. This unit leans heavily on the book from the fourth-grade Units of Study series, *Boxes and Bullets: Personal and Persuasive Essays*, and we recommend borrowing this book from a colleague when teaching this unit. The second opinion unit in this book, "Literary and Comparative Essays," helps children transfer all they've learned about essay writing to writing about texts—this time defending claims about literature using text-based evidence. Both of these units are very similar to those in the fourth-grade *If…Then…Curriculum*; we've included them here for students who didn't have them in fourth grade.

If you are concerned about readying students for the CCSS' emphasis on close reading of complex texts, you will probably want to reserve a month for a unit of study on writing poetry. "Poetry Anthologies: Writing, Thinking, and Seeing More" ushers children into a study that supports connections between reading and writing and teaches writers to zoom in on craft and its relation to meaning. In this unit, children play with language and study mentor texts as they learn to use poetry to convey specific themes and messages. "Journalism" is an old favorite, a unit in which students develop the ability to write concisely, clearly, and with purposeful organization. It won't be long before your students are running around, writing notebook in hand, looking for the next great lead for an article! We included this exceptional enrichment unit, as well as the poetry unit, in both the fourth-grade and fifth-grade *If…Then…Curriculum* books; if your students have had these units last year, you may want to adapt them this year. And finally, "Fantasy" has the power to transform students' writing and bring narrative writing to a whole new level. This second enrichment unit will immerse your class in the world of heroes, wizards, and magic, all the while pushing you and your students to synthesize the writing skills they have learned throughout the year.

Part One: Alternate and Additional Units

The Personal and Persuasive Essay

Creating Boxes and Bullets and Argument Structures for Essay Writing

RATIONALE/INTRODUCTION

The Common Core State Standards have helped to ignite new interest in a kind of writing that goes by various names: opinion, review, essay, editorial, persuasive, expository. Writers who have grown up in Reading and Writing Project writing workshops will have progressed through a spiral curriculum in opinion writing, and when this unit begins, these writers will be poised to work toward the Common Core requirements for this grade level (and beyond).

This unit is aligned to the fourth-grade unit of study *Boxes and Bullets: Personal and Persuasive Essays*. In fact, if you are choosing to teach this unit, we strongly recommend borrowing the fourth-grade book from one of your colleagues. If your students did not have the opportunity to cycle through this unit of study last year (or if their on-demand opinion writing shows significant gaps), we recommend teaching this unit before venturing on to either *Shaping Texts: From Essay or Narrative to Memoir* or *The Research-Based Argument Essay*. This unit is designed to give students strong footing in the art of essay writing, with a particular eye toward helping prime students to write on-demand, structured, thesis-driven, flash-draft essays.

Before preparing students for the opinion and argument work called for in the fifth-grade Common Core State Standards, you'll first want to consider which of the precursory skills and strategies they are missing. If you are following the Units of Study series in your school, in third grade, your writers should have learned to introduce a topic and state an opinion; list reasons; use linking words such as *because*, *therefore*, *since*, and *for example*; and give a concluding statement. By fourth grade, writers are asked and taught to introduce a topic or text *"clearly"* and provide some contextual information rather than simply stating an opinion as the introduction. Fourth-graders must also "create an organizational structure in which related ideas are grouped," meaning that they need to categorize the facts and details they are gathering. In addition, fourth-graders must support reasons with facts and details, for the first time being held accountable for elaborating on and explaining their reasons with specific evidence. They must provide a concluding section related to the opinion, meaning that their conclusion must offer closure to the piece in a way that offers final thoughts. And fourth-graders must use linking words to connect their opinions and reasons, employing terms such as *for instance*, *in addition to*, and *for example*. If your fifth-graders are missing any of these key skills, this unit will help to teach these and more.

A SUMMARY OF THE BENDS IN THE ROAD FOR THIS UNIT

In Bend I (Grow Compelling Ideas in Writer's Notebooks), you will begin by supporting children in writing personal essays that are structured in a main claim/supportive examples or reasons fashion.

In Bend II (Develop Essays), students will develop their personal essays. They will gather evidence in the form of stories and lists, organize their materials, flash-draft, revise, and edit, ending the bend by again assessing their work.

In Bend III (Raise the Quality of Your Essay Writing: Go through the Cycle with Greater Independence and Write Persuasive Essays), after less than three weeks of work on personal essays, the focus of the unit will shift to persuasive essays, probably written around the same topic as the personal essay. The work with persuasive essays proceeds more quickly, with students transferring and applying all they have learned with greater independence. As students begin to take themselves through the process, they will be undertaking work of higher cognitive demand and moving to higher levels of DOK. Let your writers decide how to take themselves through the process using all they have already learned—with minimal to no scaffolding from you. This will allow you to continue to teach into what they need as they take charge of their own learning.

   We can't stress enough how crucial it is that your students develop their confidence as essay writers and strengthen their expository writing muscles. Your students will be writing about personal topics, but that does not necessarily mean that they will be writing about topics of great personal significance. It does mean, however, that they will be choosing topics that they know well and can write well about. In this way, the focus of this unit becomes powerful expository writing, not research or collecting information on unfamiliar topics. This unit becomes about the structure and organization of essays. Later in the year, when your students encounter *The Research-Based Argument Essay* unit, they will be well primed to gather evidence and write to support their ideas, having gained the essential foundations of essay writing.

BEND I: GROW COMPELLING IDEAS IN WRITER'S NOTEBOOKS

To start the unit, we suggest you begin in a slightly different, more scaffolded way. To help your students internalize the form and voice of the personal essay, we suggest you lead them in a guided practice session in which you and the class co-create a quick personal essay on a shared topic (e.g., "I love ice cream."), with each student or each partnership writing a version of the essay, doing this work "in-the-air" first, and only later on the page. After saying aloud to each other the exact words that they might put onto the page, receiving coaching in each paragraph of that essay, students disperse to put that in-the-air text onto the page and then complete it. We expect that this initial flash-essay and others like it will be very rudimentary because students' abilities are not yet well developed.

Channel students to write to learn.

Following this initial work, you will support writers to work with great investment for almost two weeks on a personal essay. Plan to devote three or four days (and evenings and weekends, hopefully) to helping your students experience what it means to be the sort of writers who grow compelling, provocative ideas through using their writer's notebooks.

In *Boxes and Bullets: Personal and Persuasive Essays*, the minilessons encourage students to take a few days to roam around through their lives and their thinking, generating lots of entries (often three or four in one day's writing workshop) about a whole host of topics. Then, at the end of the week, students zoom in on one sentence-long idea that becomes their thesis statement for an essay. In that version of this unit, all the early entry writing ends up being valuable only as a way for writers to practice living as the kind of writers who grow compelling ideas in writer's notebooks; all that a writer takes from the entry-generating phase of the unit is a sentence or two.

You'll find that if students begin the unit with a general sense of the topic or terrain they want to mine and then use the entry-generating strategies to mine that area, the entry-writing phase allows writers to generate insights and anecdotes that stand a chance of becoming part of the essay they eventually write. It is not usually difficult for students to recognize the big topics of their lives: tensions between the student and a sibling, the months spent at summer camp, the joy and pressure of soccer, the lure of a particular video game.

One strategy that writers find particularly helpful is to list people who matter to them and then ideas they have about these people. If a student's grandmother has been growing elderly before the student's eyes, she might jot "Nana" and then list big ideas she has about her: "It is hard to watch the strongest person in your life become needy, my grandmother is teaching me that few things matter more than family ties . . ." After listing ideas in such a manner, writers can either shift to collecting Small Moment stories related to one of those ideas or they can take one of those ideas and generate new thinking around it (e.g., "I've been think-ing how our whole family is there for Nana and this makes me see that we are stronger than anything. We are like glue. When one of us needs something, the rest of us rush over. Like, our family doesn't let Nana get lonely . . .").

Another strategy that might appeal to some writers is to take an object related to a topic (a backpack, say, for a writer writing about homework) and then jot ideas the writer has about that object. To demon-strate this strategy, show writers they can again write before they have an idea of what they will say, using free-writing to generate ideas, and show them they can again use phrases such as "The thought I have about this is . . . " or "This makes me realize . . . " The student who has decided to write about homework and who focuses on his backpack might write that he is overwhelmed by the weight of his backpack. His writing might then take a turn and address the way that homework is now overwhelming his life. This can lead to yet more related thoughts in a stream-of-consciousness sort of way. Once a writer gets started writing about an idea, he needs to roll it out in his mind and on the page. The goal, for now, is not especially wonderful writing; it's writing to learn.

To that end, it is important to emphasize that when students are writing entries to grow ideas, their entries will not look like miniature essays. That is, the student writing about the weight of his backpack may have rambled from writing about the weight of the backpack to remembering olden days when life was easier to topics about free time. During this phase of the unit, your emphasis will be on teaching writers to free-write in their notebooks. The goal is to help kids realize the value of writing at length without preconceived content, trusting that original, interesting, provocative ideas will surface as they go along. You will want to encourage them to look at examples of free-writing (either yours or examples from previous students) and inquire into what makes for strong writing of this type.

Your writers might notice that free-writing is not just about big ideas, but it also contains precise examples and small stories to illustrate those ideas. Push students to try out what they notice in their own writing, charging them with moving fluidly back and forth between grappling with abstract notions and showing these through concrete details. Your writers might also notice that strong free-writing tries to explore thoughts that are not always easy to address. You will also help your students reach for the precise words to capture their thoughts and, for your most advanced students, to use metaphors for thoughts that don't easily fit into ordinary words.

Help students push initial thinking.

As students write entries in which they attempt to grow ideas around their chosen topics, you'll want to be ready to help them with any problems they encounter. You will be apt to find that students struggle to write at any length when they are writing about their ideas. A student writes, "I feel like homework is taking over all my free time. I don't have time to play outside any more. I miss the evenings when I used to play basketball in the park." But then, the writer stops. What else is there to say? It's far easier to write at length when one is chronicling what one did first, next, next, and next. But when one is writing what one thinks, the well of thoughts on any one topic can go dry. For writers who struggle to elaborate when they are writing about ideas, it might be helpful to be ready to give them tools, such as thought prompts, to push past their first thoughts Once a student records an idea, the student can use a thought prompt to get himself or herself saying more.

You'll find that thought prompts such as "The thought I have about this is . . . ," "In other words . . . ," "That is . . . ," "The surprising thing about this is . . . ," "This makes me realize . . . ," and "To add on . . . " can all help your students to extend their first ideas and use writing as a way of thinking.

The trick is to push students to *truly* develop their thinking on the page. It is helpful to tell students that thought prompts are a way not just to put words on the page, but to *think new things*. It will help if we demonstrate explicitly how these thought prompts ask us to think by positioning ourselves as "the thinkers" and the students as "the prompters." For example, if you started with an idea like "My bike let me get away from home," you'd begin by thinking aloud whatever thoughts you already had about that idea. "My bike let me get away from home. It made me feel older, like I was a teenager even when I was just a kid." The trick here is that whenever you get stuck and can't think of anything else to say (to write-in-the-air), then another person hands you a thought prompt, a sentence starter such as "In other words . . . " You repeat that sentence starter and keep talking (about the original idea.) "My bike let me get away from home. It made me feel older, like I was a teenager even when I was just a kid. In other words, getting a bike was part of growing up, and of growing away from my family." If you again pause, as if your well of thoughts is temporarily dry, someone might help you prime your thinking with another thought prompt. "The surprising thing about this is . . . "

You can set writers up to do this work with partners, where one partner is the thinker and one is the prompter, and they mimic your demonstration. Of course, then students will need to go on to do this work on their own in their notebooks, serving as their own prompters, by taking thought prompts (or sentence starters) from a list and using them to keep themselves thinking and writing. All of this work will help later on in the unit when you ask kids to elaborate on their thinking as they draft.

Once students have found the topics that matter in their lives, you can show them that it is powerful to reread their entries and their published narratives, asking, "What bigger idea might this entry be about?" In your minilesson, for example, you might reread an entry of your own writing. Perhaps at first you just reread it, and mutter, "I don't see an idea here. It is just about [whatever]." Then show students that instead of just flicking the page of your notebook to another entry, hoping that next, one has ideas right on the surface, you instead do some work to generate ideas. After looking somewhat blankly at an entry you have written, you might pick up your pen, shrug as if you are totally unsure if this is going to yield something because as you start writing, you have nothing in mind to say. Then reread the entry, muttering it to yourself, and when you come to the end, write, "The thought I have about this is . . . " and then keep writing, without a clear path for your thoughts. Show students that thoughts surface as you keep your pen moving. You may be writing "off of" the entry, writing a paragraph at the end of the entry, or you may be jotting notes in the margins of your entry, annotating it. Either way, this is fast note-taking writing, where the goal is not to write well but to find the terrain and the insights that can become an umbrella idea or topic for your upcoming work on a personal essay.

Remember, this work on elaborating and the strategies for generating thinking will all be shoehorned into a very small number of days early in the unit. You will probably only teach one or two strategies for generating ideas and anecdotes. You can teach other strategies as small-group work or use them to support your conferring. Of course, if you teach a particular strategy for generating essay entries, this doesn't mean the entire class needs to use that strategy! By now, students should be accustomed to selecting the strategy that works best for them on any given occasion, drawing on their growing repertoire. That is, the strategy you introduce in a minilesson on a particular day need not be that day's assignment for all students. Your students, of course, can also think of their own ways to collect ideas and anecdotes.

Guide students as they choose a topic and develop a thesis.

By the end of the fourth or fifth day of this unit, you'll want to teach children to choose a seed idea, also known as an opinion statement or a thesis. To support students in selecting an idea that seems especially important, fresh, and worth developing, help them to go back through their notebooks, studying what they have already written. They will consider all that might go into an essay on their topic and then reach for the exact words to express their opinion on this topic. You may suggest they rewrite this idea six or eight times, trying to consolidate it, honing it until it becomes their opinion statement.

Teach students to plan in boxes and bullets.

Once students have selected and articulated a thesis ("Getting a bike helped me grow up," for example), you will want to teach them to think about the reasons they'll include in their essays. The most accessible and common way to do this is to repeat the opinion statement ("Getting a bike helped me grow up.") and then list reasons; each reason is a bullet, a topic sentence for another portion of the essay. You may want to encourage writers to restate the thesis over and over, each time adding the transitional word *because* followed by a reason.

- Getting a bike helped me grow up **because** it allowed me to leave home.
- Getting a bike helped me grow up **because** it allowed me to see myself as "one of the gang."
- Getting a bike helped me grow up **because** it allowed me to have independence.

Repeating the stem of the thesis over and over results in a list that is full of redundancy, but this can eventually be eliminated: "Getting a bike helped me grow up because it allowed me to leave home, to see myself as one of the gang, and to have independence." Don't fret if writers don't have three bullets; two are just as good.

You will decide if you want to teach the whole class or a subset of the class another possible way to organize an essay. One alternative is a structure in which the writer writes his or her initial thought on a subject and then his or her later thought on the subject, creating an essay that is organized as a journey of thought. There are a few templates that writers have adopted and adapted when working within this frame. Try using a template like this one, for example, to capture your ideas about a bike or your mother or summers or going to bed or anything else: "I used to think . . . but now I think . . . ," "I used to think that playing with toy guns was awesome, but now I think it's scary." "I used to think that going to bed was boring, but now it is heavenly." "I used to think that a dog was just a pet, but now I realize that a dog can be part of the family." "I used to think that a bike was just a toy, but now I realize it's part of growing up." There are, of course, adaptations on that template: "If you have never . . . you probably think it is . . . but after you . . . you realize it is . . . ." "When I started to write about . . . I wanted to say . . . but after thinking more deeply about it, I realize what I really want to say is . . ." The planning for such an essay might take the following form.

I used to think that a dog was just a pet, but now I realize that a dog can be part of the family.

✓ I used to think that a dog was just a pet.
✓ Now I realize that a dog is part of the family.

Another way to help writers to write an essay that deals with multiple angles on one idea (which correlates to higher-level work in Webb's Depth of Knowledge) is to suggest that writers can build the essay around the idea "My thoughts about _____ are complicated." This essay, then, can proceed to say, "On the one hand, I think . . ." and "On the other hand, I think . . ." That will work best if the two sides of the idea are parallel to each other.

My thoughts about video games are complicated.

✓ On the one hand, they distract me from other work.
✓ On the other hand, they help me make friends.

Opinion Writing Checklist

	Grade 5	NOT YET	STARTING TO	YES!	Grade 6	NOT YET	STARTING TO	YES!
	Structure				**Structure**			
Overall	I made a claim or thesis on a topic or text, supported it with reasons, and provided a variety of evidence for each reason.	☐	☐	☐	I not only staked a position that could be supported by a variety of trustworthy sources, but also built my argument and led to a conclusion in each part of my text.	☐	☐	☐
Lead	I wrote an introduction that led to a claim or thesis and got my readers to care about my opinion. I got my readers to care by not only including a cool fact or jazzy question, but also figuring out was significant in or around the topic and giving readers information about what was significant about the topic.	☐	☐	☐	I wrote an introduction that helped readers to understand and care about the topic or text. I thought backwards between the piece and the introduction to make sure that the introduction fit with the whole.	☐	☐	☐
	I worked to find the precise words to state my claim; I let readers know the reasons I would develop later.				I not only clearly stated my claim, but also named the reasons I would develop later. I also told my readers how my text would unfold.			
Transitions	I used transition words and phrases to connect evidence back to my reasons using phrases such as *this shows that.* . . .	☐	☐	☐	I used transitional phrases to help readers understand how the different parts of my piece fit together to support my argument.	☐	☐	☐
	I helped readers follow my thinking with phrases such as *another reason* and *the most important reason.* I used phrases such as *consequently* and *because of* to show what happened.	☐	☐	☐				
	I used words such as *specifically* and *in particular* in order to be more precise.	☐	☐	☐				

During this planning day, your students will each craft a thesis and several parallel supporting ideas. Teachers sometimes refer to the thesis and supporting statements or reasons as boxes and bullets.

This bend will end with students self-assessing their on-demand pieces and setting goals before they begin the process of developing an essay. You will want to involve them in using the Opinion Writing Checklist, Grades 5 and 6, to set and revise personal goals and create action plans before moving into the next part of the unit, when they will begin to develop and draft their essays.

BEND II: DEVELOP ESSAYS

In the second bend, students will develop their personal essays. They will gather evidence in the form of stories and lists, organize their materials, flash-draft, revise, and edit, ending the bend by again assessing their work.

Support students as they gather evidence.

If essay writing is new for students, it helps if students take their thesis and record it on the outside of a folder, then make smaller internal folders for each of their reasons/bullets (which later become topic sentences). The folders will house all of the facts and details the students will gather to support each of their reasons. After a few days of collecting and revising the small pile, a student will spread out the contents of each small folder, select the best material for that body paragraph, and rewrite the selected material into that body paragraph, grouping related information. This work can be done in a fashion that detours around the folders, with writers essentially developing each of their bullets on a different sheet of paper. If you bypass the folder method, your writers will not revise until they have large swatches of text, which often leads them to do little revision and therefore to not ratchet up their skills as much as they otherwise would.

If writers gather materials for two of their body paragraphs in folders, compile and organize these materials, and then draft these sections of their essays, they can repeat the process with greater independence and take themselves through developing the third section of the essay. When setting up the folders, you might explain to students that they will be using two folders to gather materials; talk to them about their third bullet at a later point in the unit. This system will also help you to move more quickly through the process of gathering materials and drafting.

To support students in gathering materials, you will want to show them that they can first collect micro-stories that illustrate their ideas. As part of this instruction, you'll also want to teach students to angle these stories to highlight and support the ideas they want to advance. Teach students that writers sometimes collect angled stories, and then give students many opportunities to practice and become proficient at this technique. They also, of course, may revise these to bring out the points they want to make. Keep in mind that during one day of a writing workshop, a student will need to collect (and ideally revise) at least three angled stories, filing these in the appropriate folder. It would most certainly not be considered a day's work for a student to write one tiny anecdote supporting one of the student's three topic sentences! Furthermore, if a student takes a day to write an anecdote illustrating one of his topic sentences, chances are that the narrative will overwhelm the rest of the essay. Generally, within essays, writers write with tight, small anecdotes. Let your students know that you expect them to fill up both of their folders within a day or two (including for homework).

After you teach students to collect mini-stories to illustrate their points, teach them that writers can also collect another type of material: lists. You may want to show students a speech like Martin Luther King's "I Have a Dream," which contains lists, or another student's work or your own text with lists, helping them to see the repetition of key phrases. Then send students off to work, reminding them to fill up their folders with a variety of materials and letting them decide whether they need to draft more mini-stories, collect a few lists, or do a little of both.

Guide students as they sort and organize material.

After two days of collecting materials, teach writers to sort through the materials in each folder, considering whether all of their evidence supports their reasons. You can model rereading one of your own mini-stories, questioning if each part of your story matches your reason, and showing students how to cut or revise the story if every bit of it does not match. Through small-group work, mid-workshop teaching, and/or shares, you can also show students how to look through folders and choose their best materials, ending with perhaps two stories and a list for one section and a longer story for another. You want to help writers streamline their materials to help them organize for drafting.

After a few sessions of gathering evidence, you can teach your writers to compile all of the diverse material they have collected to compose a draft. Teach your fifth-graders that writers put materials together first by arranging the material in an order that would make the most sense to the reader, and then using transitional words and key words from opinion statements to put the material together. You might teach them to lay out all of their material and rehearse one section with a partner, using transition words and phrases. After rehearsing their body paragraphs, you can let writers draft. Once writers have selected the most powerful and pertinent support material for each of their topic sentences, they can staple, tape, or recopy this information into a paragraph or two that support each topic sentence—the rough draft of an essay. Expect your classroom to be filled with a flurry of scissors, tape, and excitement!

If your students are especially on target and you want to add some challenges to the unit, either in your whole-class teaching or perhaps in a small group, you can teach that writers look over their material to decide the best way to use evidence to support the main point of the essay. For example, if a writer has an angled story that makes her point in an especially powerful way, she may decide to let the essay revolve mostly around that one story. She will then write (or rewrite) the story to be sure it carries the idea, mining that one story for insights and big ideas. That is, if your students are proficient enough that you want them to understand the breadth and flexibility of essays, and if they are not under any compulsion to create thesis-driven five-paragraph essays, then you'll probably want to show them that as they draft and revise their essays, they can make decisions based on the material that they have on hand. But if you want to help writers produce competent, well-structured essays quickly, you may decide not to introduce the full range of options and choices just yet.

After your writers have constructed their first two body paragraphs, you will want to teach them to go through the process again with more independence. You might explain to them that they have not made folders for their third bullet, and they can now decide if they want to make a folder. Guide them to take charge of their own writing, brainstorming with them a list of work that needs to be done. Then set a deadline of perhaps a day or two, during which time they need to gather evidence, organize materials, and draft their third body paragraph.

As students work through this process, you might show them how to create an introduction and conclusion, work that is highlighted in the Common Core State Standards. According to the CCSS, opinion writers should introduce a topic and create an organizational structure in which related ideas are grouped logically to support the writer's purpose (W.5.1a). Thus, you can teach your writers that essayists use introductions and conclusions as a way to highlight for readers what the essay will be about, the logical order it will follow, and why it is important.

In another session (or perhaps tucked into the previous session if you are short on time or your students' writing is fairly proficient structurally), teach your writers that one way essay writers revise is to read through each section, making sure the information in that section all goes together and all supports that part of the essay. This would be a good time for your fifth-graders to rely on their writing partnerships, studying each other's drafts to make sure all of the information fits together in each section.

You can wrap up this first part of the unit by supporting your students in polishing their essays, editing for mechanics and spelling, and perhaps holding a small celebration that might be a longer share session one day. You might end this bend with a tip that is angled toward transference, reminding your writers that you are teaching them critical moves that they will use as essay writers not just today but always.

BEND III: RAISE THE QUALITY OF YOUR ESSAY WRITING: GO THROUGH THE CYCLE WITH GREATER INDEPENDENCE AND WRITE PERSUASIVE ESSAYS

In this last bend, you will support your students as you teach them how to move from personal to persuasive essays and raise the level of their writing.

When students are writing personal essays, for the most part they are writing about ideas that no one can really argue with. Because the source of most material for this essay comes from the writer's experience, a classmate or reader cannot really say "That's not true." In other words, if I write an essay driven by a thesis that says, "Being an only child can be lonely," and I support that idea with stories of my own loneliness, I remove the possibility for argument, because it would be bizarre for someone to tell me my experience is mistaken. This personal work is important because as you are teaching your students the root moves of essay writing, you want to make sure that they are focused primarily on the writing work—the logical progression of support for a thesis—rather than the art of argument.

However, once you have reached a point where the foundations of essay writing are in place, it is important that you then carry the work forward into argument-driven essays that strive not only to name experiences and ideas, but that also try to convince the reader that something is true. To begin this work, you might want to gather your students in the meeting area, refocusing their attention on this slightly new bend and building their enthusiasm for the new work ahead. Tell your class that because they have done such a stellar job of writing personal essays, they are ready now to learn something that every citizen of the world must learn: the power of argument. "Writers," you might say, "today we are going to begin to be very brave. Yesterday we were content to write essays in which we simply told the world what we thought or how we felt. You have become writers of ideas, and you have learned to find stories that support your ideas. Today, we are going to learn how to uncover ideas that we believe in ourselves and that we think other people should believe, too. Ideas that other people—people in this class even—might disagree with. This takes bravery, and I know that you are all very brave indeed."

You might then explain to your students that when you look at some of the ideas you had during the personal essay unit, ideas like "Being an only child is difficult," you realize that no one could really argue about that issue because it is so personal to you. You can model for them how you begin to collect more persuasive ideas by asking yourself some questions, such as "How could the world change for the better?" or "Is there anything that people do that I think is wrong or unfair?" or "Some people think . . . but I think . . . " Your students will see your ideas transform from clear but personal statements into bold, persuasivemottos, such as "People should stop putting only children down," or "Parents of only children should make sure that their kids are involved in lots of groups" or "Some people think that being an only child is bad for you, but I think that it is the best way to grow up, even if it is hard sometimes." You will want to encourage your students to branch off into other directions from their original idea as well, using these persuasive questions to help them generate a long list of things they wish they could change in the world.

You may see notebook pages spilling over with strong opinions after these kinds of lessons. "No one should be mean to people." "Cats are better than dogs." "Some people think video games are bad for you, but I think they can be good, too." Inevitably, as your students share these ideas with the class, you will hear grumbles of disagreement. You might even be surprised at the vehemence with which your children voice their disagreement. "No, they are not!" and "That's not true!" will be common refrains, and when you hear these words, you can quiet your class and let them know that they have arrived in the land of argument.

In this bend of the unit, we aim not only to introduce students to the art of argument but also to support them in gaining independence in writing essays. This bend then, in addition to helping students learn the moves of persuasion, also reminds students of all that they have learned and pushes them to transfer and apply that learning as they write essays with greater independence. You will want to remind students of the resources that exist to help them—the charts, checklists, mentor texts, demonstration pieces, and so on.

As students go through the process, you will want to raise the level of the work they are doing by teaching strategies for gathering a greater variety of evidence. Remind your class that when writing personal essays, they leaned on their own stories; in persuasive writing, these personal stories and the stories of others became great backup for their thinking. Mentor texts provide inspiration for other types of material children will want to collect. For example, many well-written pieces of persuasive writing rely on an image that functions as a central metaphor. You could also teach children that nothing is more persuasive than facts. Writers who want to convince their readers use precise information, and this could mean that a teacher might teach students how to use the Internet to search for precise evidence, such as a statistic or a quotation to illustrate a topic sentence. Your decision will depend on several factors, including time and access to technology.

Any of these strategies can help your students lift the level of their writing as they flash-draft essays or as revision strategies later on. Some may work as whole-class lessons, while others can serve as your small-group instruction or conference work.

You may gather your students around you again, congratulating them on the work they have done so far, and then saying, "Writers, you are at a critical point in your writing life. You have good arguments about great ideas. The problem is that a good argument may not win the debate. We need *great* arguments. And the way to make your arguments great is to make sure there are no holes in your arguments." Certainly here you could weave a connection to the times children have argued with their parents over a late night or new toy, pointing out that to convince a parent to bend, the argument needs to be airtight, not just good enough.

You will want to teach students to rehearse by trying to convince partners of their opinions and let partners act as critical friends, letting writers know how convincing they found the evidence. Then partners might offer suggestions for whether writers need more evidence or whether they need to better connect the evidence to their reasons. You will teach your students that this work can uncover gaps in evidence and allow writers to know what further evidence they need to gather to be as convincing as possible.

As students go through the writing process, you will want to highlight a few revision goals along the way. Show writers how to unpack their evidence, linking each piece to their opinion and reasons. Simply teaching students to include more evidence may not be the best revision lesson here. Instead, you can demonstrate some craft work, teaching your students that writers include more than just facts and details, that they also explain how those facts and details are connected to the thesis or to the supporting point.

You can teach students common phrases such as "This shows . . . " or "This proves . . . " to show how each piece of evidence supports their reasons. Then let them go back to revise not only their current pieces but also all the essay drafts they have written. You can remind writers to use language that is domain-specific to the topics of their essays and, in addition, to include phrases, words, and clauses such as *consequently* and *specifically*, as the Common Core expects (W.5.1c).

Most importantly, teach students that writers reread and revise, taking their readers into account. Teach them that writers pretend to be their own readers. They step outside of themselves, pick up the text as if they have never seen it before, and read it. They notice the sections that are convincing and those that make them flick the paper away in disbelief. They notice where the draft loses energy and where it makes the reader feel skeptical. Of course, revision is another time for studying mentor texts. Teach students to go back to their pieces and try out the kinds of rhetorical gestures and "zingers" that drive home the point in a quotable way, using mentor texts as models. If your students have done outside research, you can teach them to paraphrase that information here, being sure to show them how to cite their sources either inside of the text or as a separate works-cited page.

CELEBRATE PERSUASIVE WRITING: FINDING A PLACE FOR OUR OPINIONS IN THE WORLD

You may chose to make this publication a bigger deal than other essay celebrations by leaning on the persuasive elements and holding debates, filming essays as speeches, or having students create podcasts around their work. If you have been pushing your students to write as persuasively as possible, you may also want to help them make a difference in the world by trying to put their writing into the hands of people that could be changed by it. However you celebrate, be sure to remind your students of all they have learned in this weighty unit. In their rigor and stamina, they will have developed their essay-writing muscles exponentially.

EDITING AND WORD STUDY TO SUPPORT THE WRITING WORKSHOP

Throughout this unit, you will want to focus on conventions that help students to produce readable writing. Most importantly, remind students to transfer and apply all they already know about conventions to this part of their drafting work. You will want to say to your students, "We don't wait until we are finished writing to go back and check the spelling of words we should already know by heart. Instead, we take a little time while writing to make sure these words are spelled correctly." Then remind students of the strategies they have learned to check spelling, such as glancing at the word wall, trying out words a few times, and considering parts. Teach your students that when they use the word wall, they should take a pretend "photograph" of the whole word, write the *entire* word as best they can without peeking, and then check it one more time against the word wall. They should *not* try to look at the word and copy one letter at a time; words are learned by practicing the whole word. The goal is not to slow down their writing but to help them to remember to incorporate the correct spelling as they write. By the end of fifth grade, students are expected to spell all grade-appropriate words correctly. You will want to focus your teaching on making the use of their repertoire of spelling strategies a fluid part of their writing process.

This time of year is also a good time to do a quick, informal assessment by looking across kids' independent writing to see which high-frequency words many children continue to misspell. Even if you already introduced those words as word wall words, you may revisit them again and again until most of your children spell them correctly in their independent writing.

Now that your year is well underway, you might want to raise the bar on your students' grammar expectations. In the exploration of essay writing, you might have students revisit sentence types as a jumping-off point to work on sentence combining. Many students have a difficult time recognizing that a sentence can be simple (The cat <u>ate</u> the fish.), compound (The cat <u>took</u> the fish, and she <u>buried</u> it in the garden.), or complex (The cat <u>ate</u> the fish because he <u>could not dig</u> a hole in the concrete.). The work begun in this unit will lay the foundation for more challenging work ahead.

This is also the perfect time to revisit paragraphing of new ideas. Informational writing provides an opportunity to remind children about when and where to use paragraphs to signal a new idea. In addition, students are ready to investigate abstract vocabulary that signals connections (*and, thus, furthermore, rather*), compares or contrasts a viewpoint (*however, on the other hand*) or advances an idea (interjections: *or, yet*). This inquiry work might begin in read-aloud, where you could begin to tune your students' ears to hear the words that signal agreement, viewpoint, or interjection and collect the words on a chart by category. Children can use this resource tool when writing notebook entries or drafts.

Information Writing
Feature Articles on Topics of Personal Expertise

RATIONALE/INTRODUCTION

If your fifth-graders have not been part of writing workshops prior to now and have not had any experience writing information texts, then you may want to teach this unit, because it invites children to write feature articles in ways that align with all the CCSS for fifth grade. The fact that students will be writing on topics they know well rather than researching topics that are important in their curriculum means they'll have the advantage of being able to draw upon personal expertise. Consequently, students' focus can be on all the challenges of this kind of writing. After you teach this unit, your students will likely be ready for the demanding work of *The Lens of History: Research Reports*.

The genre of information writing is remarkably wide open. Crystallize in your mind an information text. To do this, your mind probably casts over the options. You consider pamphlets, feature articles, nonfiction books, websites, textbooks, research reports, encyclopedias, atlases, guide books, blogs, and recipes. You think, "Of all these many forms, is there one that captures the essence of information writing?" Chances are good that no single image surfaces.

The Common Core State Standards highlight the importance of this genre, naming it informative/explanatory or explanatory writing and describing it as writing that is designed to "examine a topic and convey information and ideas clearly." Just as a term like *memoir* means very different things to different people, so, too, *information writing* can be thought of as a tent-like term that covers a wide collection of forms of writing.

It is important that you decide on the kind of information writing you will teach and the form it will take. In planning for this genre, we decided to exclude all of the forms of information writing that have a narrative structure, settling on a definition of information writing that is expository in design. This doesn't mean an information text won't contain stories—it will—but there will be an infrastructure (an outline, almost) into which a story is set, and the entire text will not be a single story. There is also the question of whether persuasive letters, speeches, reviews, and petitions will be regarded as information writing and whether literary and historical essays will qualify as information writing. Because the Common Core State Standards name three kinds of writing and do so by separating argument/opinion writing and information writing (with narrative being the third), we decided that we will not treat thesis-driven texts that advance a claim as information writing. Of course, an information text can contain a section that has an essay-like structure, but the text itself will not all advance a single, overarching thesis. We also acknowledge that at the highest levels, some information writing will resemble argument writing. But, then, some information writing will resemble poetry as well!

This unit channels students to write feature articles, a common form of information writing, on topics of personal expertise. The driving structure of these feature articles is apt to be categories and subcategories: topics and subtopics that are signaled with headings and subheadings and with accompanying portals for information, including glossaries and text boxes or sidebars and diagrams, charts, graphs, and other visuals. This unit, then, teaches students to write within one particular template for information writing. That template is illustrated in the mentor texts that we highlight. A handful of qualities of strong information writing are taught with vigor and clarity, and students' progress toward producing this sort of writing is tracked, supported, and expected. The results have been as dramatic as the results we commonly see from units of study in narrative writing.

MANDATES, TESTS, STANDARDS

A key component of this genre is structure. According to the CCSS, fifth-grade information writers should group related information *logically* (W.5.2a). This is a notable progression from fourth grade, in which writers are asked to group related information into paragraphs and sections (W.4.2a). The assumption, of course, is that fifth-graders are already able to group information, as required of fourth-graders, but now the expectation is that they organize the information both within and across sections in a way that best furthers their purpose. Additionally, the Common Core urges fifth-grade writers to move toward a cohesive structure through the use of linking words and phrases that not only connect information within sections, but that also show relationships between pieces of information (W.5.2c).

A second crucial quality of good information writing is elaboration. The CCSS state that fifth-grade writers should be able to develop topics with facts, definitions, concrete details, quotations, or other information and examples related to the topic (W.5.2b), as well as illustrations and even multimedia when these are appropriate (W.5.2a). Indeed, good information writers incorporate a wealth of specific information, including the terms and definitions that are specific to their topics. The Common Core State Standards refer to these terms as "domain-specific vocabulary" (W.5.2d) and expect fifth-grade writers to incorporate such terminology, along with precise language, as part of informing readers about their topics.

In this unit, students will work toward creating well-structured, well-elaborated, engaging feature articles. One of the rules of thumb in writing is that a writer can only engage readers in a topic if the writer is engaged in that topic. The unit, then, assumes that students are writing about self-chosen topics of great personal interest. It could be that students know about subtopics they have studied during content area instruction, and they can write with engagement and authority on a subtopic that falls under the purview of their social studies or science curriculum. However, if students are just embarking on a social studies unit and know only the barest outline about that topic, they would not be apt to write well on that topic. It is likely, then, that many students will write on topics of personal interest and experience.

Teachers wanting to learn more about information writing can refer to the rich tradition of work in nonfiction writing done by leaders in the field, such as Don Murray, E. B. White, Roy Peter Clark, William Zinsser, and Elizabeth Lyon.

ASSESSMENT

We recommend that you spend one class period conducting an on-demand information writing assessment before launching this unit. You will find the prompt for this on-demand assessment in the book *Writing Pathways: Performance Assessments and Learning Progressions, Grades K–5*. You will give them the prompt and then, the following day, you will provide them with sixty minutes, or one writing workshop, to show what they know about information writing.

Then, refer to the Information Writing Checklist, Grades 5 and 6 to study your writers' work. Your fifth-graders have had plenty of experience with information writing already, and most will be ready for increasing levels of sophistication in this work. If your students demonstrate that they have mastered most of the big work of level 4, such as introducing a topic clearly, grouping information, and providing a variety of elaboration, then they are certainly ready to undertake the challenges outlined in this unit.

Many teachers find that after students do an initial on-demand piece of writing, it can be helpful to give them an intensive reminder about information writing and then allow them to spend a single day rewriting their on-demand piece, from top to bottom. The new work they produce can then be assessed using the information checklist. This allows you to assess what students know how to do with the barest minimum of instruction and also to assess what is easily within their grasp with just a few reminders.

This on-demand writing will help you know where your students fall in a trajectory of writing development and will help you set your sights on very clear next steps. It will also help students realize that

Information Writing Checklist

	Grade 5	YES!	STARTING TO	NOT YET	Grade 6	YES!	STARTING TO	NOT YET
	Structure				**Structure**			
Overall	I used different kinds of information to teach about the subject. Sometimes I included little essays, stories, or "how-to" sections in my writing.	☐	☐	☐	I conveyed ideas and information about a subject. Sometimes I incorporated essays, explanations, stories, or procedural passages into my writing.	☐	☐	☐
Lead	I wrote an introduction that helped readers get interested in and understand the subject. I let readers know the subtopics I would be developing later as well as the sequence.	☐	☐	☐	I wrote an introduction in which I interested readers, perhaps with a quote or significant fact. I may have included my own ideas about the topic. I let readers know the subtopics that I would develop later and how my text will unfold.	☐	☐	☐
Transitions	When I wrote about results, I used words and phrases like *consequently, as a result,* and *because of this.* When I compared information, I used words and phrases such as *in contrast, by comparison,* and *especially.* In narrative parts, I used phrases that go with stories such as *a little later* and *three hours later.* In the sections that stated an opinion, I used words such as *but the most important reason, for example,* and *consequently.*	☐	☐	☐	I used transition words to help my readers understand how different bits of information and different parts of my writing fit together.	☐	☐	☐
					The writer used transitions such as *for instance, in addition, therefore, such as, because of, as a result, in contrast to, unlike, despite,* and *on the other hand* to help connect ideas, information, and examples and to compare, contrast, and imply relationships.	☐	☐	☐
Ending	I wrote a conclusion in which I restated the main points and may have offered a final thought or question for readers to consider.	☐	☐	☐	I wrote a conclusion in which I restated my important ideas and offered a final insight or implication for readers to consider.	☐	☐	☐

information writing is well within their grasp and not something that requires days and weeks of preparation. Most teachers who have done the on-demand assessment have been pleasantly surprised by how much students bring into this unit of study and by the volume of writing students are able to produce in just one day's writing workshop. The work that students produce in the on-demand situation becomes the baseline, and you can increase expectations as the unit progresses.

A SUMMARY OF THE BENDS IN THE ROAD FOR THIS UNIT

In Bend I (Organize Information and Plan a Feature Article), you will begin by teaching students that information writers plan different ways their articles can go, first by coming up with big categories, then adding examples and important terms to each. Students will learn the different ways topics can be divided, then move on to some outside research. Students will learn to think of each category as a "file," storing information into each, then taking a look at them to see what needs further revision. This first bend will likely take a week.

In Bend II (Draft and Revise in Ways that Teach Others), you will teach students that writers plan sections just as they plan whole books, keeping organization and order in mind as they draft using headings and subheadings. Writers will continually revise, improving their work through elaboration strategies. You will then teach writers linking words and phrases to keep all their information together. Continue to encourage writers to conduct outside research. Writers also learn to keep certain things in mind, like using an expert vocabulary, writing for an audience, and writing a thoughtful conclusion. Students will likely cycle through the drafting and revising process for several days.

In Bend III (Revise, Format, and Edit to Best Teach Readers), you and your students will assess their drafts using the checklist. Writers will incorporate text features into their drafts. Writers will also begin editing, paying attention to spelling, and setting off definitions using commas. Finally, authors will learn to use phrases like *in addition* and *furthermore* to advance an idea. You may want to keep this bend short and focused.

In Bend IV (Bring What They Learn from Long, Intense Projects to Quick-Writes), you might have your students quickly switch to writing an information book about another topic, maybe in social studies or science. Students can then turn back to their revision work. Follow publication with a celebration where you invite your students to teach a younger class you have invited.

GETTING READY

Most teachers find that mentor texts can be powerful co-teachers in any writing unit. This is especially true in information writing, when clear examples of structure, elaboration, and other hallmarks of the genre are key.

When choosing mentor texts for this unit, you will want to choose texts that highlight the things you plan to teach, such as information organized into categories, a table of contents, accessible text features, and examples of embedded domain vocabulary. And, of course, most of your mentors will be feature articles. Further, you'll want to make sure your mentor texts are accessible to your students and are examples of quality writing. While there is no magic text that will be able to encompass everything you might want to teach, we have found that many of the feature articles in the *Junior Scholastic Magazine* are wonderful mentors. *Cobblestone* magazine has wonderful feature articles about American history. *Ranger Rick*, the magazine of the National Wildlife Federation, contains articles that can be good mentor texts, as well. What is important when searching for possible mentor articles is that you look for articles that are not more than six to ten pages in length, because that will more closely match the volume expectation for your writers' end products.

In addition to using feature articles as mentors, you could also use information books to highlight and reinforce some of the universal qualities of good information writing. A few we recommend are *The Rock We Eat: Salt*, by Laura Layton Strom (Scholastic Shockwave series); *Votes for Women*, by Ann M. Rossi (National Geographic Reading Expeditions series); and Sy Montgomery's *Scientists in the Field* series, particularly *Kakapo Rescue: Saving the World's Strangest Parrot*. Additionally, you might choose to use your science and social studies texts as mentors. Joy Hakim's series *A History of Us* is particularly well-structured and well-elaborated, with lively anecdotes and interesting text features.

No matter what text (or texts) you ultimately decide upon, most teachers find it helpful to introduce the text in a read-aloud a few days before the unit begins and let students respond first as readers. Allow them to talk over fascinating facts and central ideas with their partners, argue points that seem worth arguing, and in general, respond as readers to the text. This is important because students will want to hold on to the effect a strongly written text can have on readers, and we also want students to feel so familiar with the text that they can focus on the writing, not the content.

Then return to the text and guide the students to explore it as writers. You might say something like, "As you all know, we are going to start creating our own feature articles soon. I thought it would be helpful for us to study what makes up a strong feature article."

Then, depending on how experienced you and your students are with mentor texts and/or information writing, you might choose to study the text as a whole class or to have the students break up into small groups and study it that way.

Generate Ideas for Expert Topics to Prepare for Feature Article Writing

In the week or so before the unit begins, channel your writers to live like authors of feature articles, carefully studying the subjects they know about for possible topics. Teach kids a few different generating strategies, such as naming topics on which they have expertise, topics they could teach to others. These topics could come from their personal lives, from subjects they have studied in school, from stories they have seen on the news, read in papers, or heard others discussing. Elizabeth Lyon, author of *A Writer's Guide to Nonfiction*, talks about the importance of information writers choosing a topic to which they feel connected. As a way to explore possible topics, Lyon suggests writers start by naming a topic in which they are interested and have some expertise, such as dogs. Then, they should quickly draft a list of facets of their experience with the topic, for example, "seeing-eye dogs, owning a rescue dog, French bulldogs . . ." After listing, they should consider which items feel the most compelling, the ones they feel have emotional impact, or "juice," as Lyon puts it.

You could also add strategies from previous units. For example, you could teach your writers to think about people and places that are meaningful to them and to generate lists of possible topics of expertise connected to these people and places. One could imagine a writer generating an idea for a topic such as the history of Apple Computers when thinking about her older brother, a computer programmer. What is paramount, of course, is that writers feel a connection to their topics. These generating activities will be quick mini-activities tucked into your day and not entire writing workshops. Just before the unit begins, you might find some time to hold minishare sessions in which you give your writers the opportunity to talk with others about the topics they are mulling over.

BEND I: ORGANIZE INFORMATION AND PLAN A FEATURE ARTICLE

It is likely that it will take your fifth-graders no time at all to generate topics of personal expertise and that you won't need to spend much time at the start of the unit teaching them to generate ideas for topics. Instead, you will be able to jump right into teaching them how information writers generate ideas for different ways their articles could go. However, if your students have not yet settled on topics, you may decide to launch the unit with one session in which they choose a topic, using some of the strategies enumerated above.

Help students prepare to teach others information about a topic.

Either way, whether your writers come to this unit with topics in hand or whether they need some time at the start to consider possible topics, part of your teaching very early on can be that information writers "try on" topics for size by teaching others all they know about the topic. On this day, which will be structured more like a shared experience than a minilesson, you could begin by demonstrating how you do this kind of work with your own topic. Show your writers how you get ready to teach by planning the big categories you'll talk about so you remember what you will say, and by coming up with a few examples and important terms you could include. You could set your fifth-graders up to try this work in small groups, teaching each other about their topics while you coach in. Remind them that when doing this teaching, it will help if writers list points across their fingers, use gestures and drama to reenact, refer to drawings and diagrams, and use an explaining voice. Later, as you debrief, you can point out the connection between good teaching and good information writing, perhaps capturing on a chart some of the teaching moves that worked particularly well, such as listing a "table of contents" in the beginning, giving lots of examples, and using illustrations or gestures. After writers have spent some time teaching each other and debriefing, you could set them up to write long and strong, fast and furious, to capture all of their teaching.

Channel students to plan and then revise a feature article.

In the next several sessions, channel your writers to plan how their articles will go, and then revise those plans right away. If your fifth-graders are experienced informational writers, they will need minimal support. If they do not have as much experience planning for information writing by organizing a topic into categories, you can teach them to think about different ways that topics can be divided, such as parts, kinds, times, or famous examples. You'll want to make sure you have your own topic of personal expertise at the ready to demonstrate how this might go. You might choose a topic that engages you, but also that will be accessible to your fifth-graders, and that would warrant some amount of research. In this write-up, we use the topic Central Park, a topic that certainly warrants research but also a topic with which many fifth-graders who live in New York City have personal experience.

Then, demonstrate how this topic could be divided in multiple ways.

Kinds: kinds of attractions, kinds of people who visit the park

Parts: sections of Central Park

Times: history of Central Park, Central Park in every season

The focus here is for children to try out different ways to divide their topic, even if some ways lack finesse. When supporting your writers as they write independently, we suggest you draw on your collection of mentor texts. For example, you might use several books to guide a small group through an inquiry on other ways information books could be organized.

Of course, you won't want your writers to spend days and days planning. You'll want to make sure they are writing with volume and stamina right from the start. You also want to make sure they are starting to collect initial information, which they will organize and elaborate upon as they draft. You might teach your fifth-graders that, early on in the process, information writers often get their ideas going and test out possible topics by writing fast and furious everything they know about their topics.

Guide students as they conduct focused research on a topic.

Additionally, you can teach your fifth-graders to conduct some preliminary research using outside sources. This is a perfect opportunity to support your fifth-graders in moving toward the Common Core expectation that they should be able to "recall relevant information from experiences or gather relevant information from print and digital sources; summarize or paraphrase information in notes and finished work, and provide a list of sources" (W.5.8). Although this unit is not a research unit, you can certainly teach your fifth-graders to conduct some quick, focused research right from the start. The Internet will be a particularly useful resource, because your writers will have such varied topics. A trip to the school or local library would likely prove helpful as well. Your students probably already know some methods for note-taking. You may want to remind them of some of these methods, such as sketching, boxes and bullets, timelines, summaries, flowcharts, and T-charts, perhaps in a mid-workshop teaching point. Of course, you'll want to remind them to keep a list of the sources they use, so they can later add them to the end of their articles.

After writers have essentially settled on plans for their books and have gathered some information, you can teach them that information writers often think of each possible chapter as a "file." Then, writers slot information that they have gathered into those files. We have found that when writers do this categorization, it often leads them to revise their plans for their whole books. Additionally, doing this work helps writers to decide which chapters are ready to be written and which will require some research. As a way to wrap up this first bend of the unit and to get kids ready for drafting, you might hold a slightly longer share session as you celebrate some of the topics kids have chosen and the ways they have decided their books will go.

BEND II: DRAFT AND REVISE IN WAYS THAT TEACH OTHERS

Just as students will choose topics cyclically throughout the entire unit, so too, writers will plan their first chapter on their fourth day or so of the unit, and then they'll plan another chapter on, say, their sixth day, and another on, say, the ninth day, and so forth. So although we address this topic in one place within this write-up, it is important for teachers to keep in mind that every writer in this unit will be continually cycling between planning, drafting, and revising a chapter and then planning another chapter.

Help students plan and organize information into parts or sections.

You might set your students up for drafting by teaching them that information writers plan sections just like they plan whole books. Writers might plan the layout of a section by thinking about different ways the subtopic could be divided into parts, about what readers would want to know, and about the order in which it makes sense to teach the information. Remind your writers that this planning should take just a few minutes and that they should get on to drafting sections, writing fast and furious. In another early drafting session, you can teach your writers to consider what "stuff" goes into each section, just as someone going on a trip thinks, "Does this item fit with the trip I'm taking?" as he packs. Writers can look over everything they are planning to put into a section and think, "Does this fit with the journey I'm taking my readers on?"

You will certainly want your fifth-graders to think about ways to organize information hierarchically within sections. Teach them to study the information they have compiled for a particular section and think, "What might the subsections be?" Next, teach them to denote this organizational structure with headings and subheadings and to begin with topic sentences that tell what the section will be about. A heading might be "Animal Lovers Welcome," in which case the topic sentence might say, "Central Park has many attractions for animal lovers." One could then imagine a subsection titled "Central Park Zoo," another titled "Central Park Conservatory," and another titled "Bird-Watching Walking Tours." Additional teaching you could do, perhaps in a small-group session, is to point out that, in more sophisticated feature articles, the headings and subheadings themselves become more sophisticated. They may use metaphor or figurative language or perhaps use quotes or sayings.

Channel students to revise and elaborate on sections with anecdotes, examples, and facts.

Young writers will need to revise—just as they will need to choose a topic and draft—continually throughout the unit. You'll teach writers a repertoire of tools for revision and reasons to revise and expect them to revise any one chapter more than once as they learn new ways to revise. Writers will need to revisit completed chapters, bringing new lenses to bear on those chapters. After teaching just a few powerful organization strategies in this bend, we suggest you shift your teaching toward elaboration. The Common Core State Standards suggest that fifth-grade information writers "develop the topic with facts, definitions, concrete details, quotations, or other information and examples related to the topic" (W.5.2b). You might want to have your writers do some inquiry work with the mentor texts you have chosen, studying these texts closely and thinking about all of the different kinds of information the authors use to teach the readers.

One thing your writers might notice is that information writers often embed anecdotes into their texts. Your writers might try this by taking what they know about Small Moment writing to craft little stories that are illustrative of whatever they are teaching. They might note, in particular, that the anecdotes in information books are *teaching* anecdotes; that is, they are angled to be illustrative of what the writer wants readers to learn about the information. For example, in the text *The Rock We Eat: Salt*, Laura Strom embeds a narrative about a king's daughter who asked that a meal be prepared without salt to illustrate the importance of this precious mineral. She only includes details that teach readers about the importance of salt, a helpful tip when embedding narratives into information writing.

Information writers also often include examples. A writer composing a book about guide dogs might write, "Guide dogs are very valuable to the people they help," and then follow this with "Guide dogs help people with countless everyday activities, such as crossing the street, making meals, and even using the ATM." Writers also often elaborate by comparing whatever they've just said to something that the reader may know. For example, "Guide dogs go through extensive training before they are ready to live with someone who is vision impaired. Their training is similar to the boot camp that soldiers go through when they join the army."

As writers do this inquiry work, you can generate a chart with a list of all of the ways that information writers elaborate, such as concrete facts, examples, anecdotes, lists, comparisons, important terms and definitions, and descriptions. As a way to align your chart with higher levels of Webb's Depths of Knowledge (DOK), you could include not only the kind of elaboration (e.g., anecdotes), but also an example from a mentor text, along with a before-and-after example from a student writer, showing the particular elaboration strategy in action.

Teach students to use linking words to connect information.

Next, teach your writers some linking words and phrases to glue all of this rich information together. You can begin by teaching and charting the linking words the CCSS suggests for fifth-graders, *in contrast* and *especially* (W.5.2c), while of course, reviewing linking words they learned as fourth-graders: *another*, *for example*, *also*, and *because* (W.4.2c). You can add others to ramp up the level of thinking work that your writers do, as well as to support varying text structures they might be using, such as *on the other hand*, *consequently*, and *therefore*. We have found this is a great time for students to draw on their nonfiction reading work. You can teach them to identify words and phrases that authors use to connect pieces of information in published texts and to use these in their own writing. For example, Ann Rossi, author of *Votes for Women* (National Geographic), uses the linking word *meanwhile* to demonstrate the connection between two historical events: the Civil War and the creation of the National Women's Loyal League. Rossi's use of the word *meanwhile* shows that the creation of the League grew out of the changing role of women in society during the time of the Civil War.

The main purpose of information writing is to teach, and the main purpose of opinion writing is to offer ideas or opinions. However, there are times when these two forms of writing blend. You can teach your fifth-graders that information writers teach not just with regurgitation and compilation of facts, but also with some ideas about those facts. Writers can study a carefully selected portion of your mentor text and notice the ways the writer embeds his or her ideas along with the facts. You can teach your writers to go back to their notebooks and use them as a tool for generating ideas. They can draw on prompts they use to grow ideas in essay writing, such as "I notice . . . ," "The thought I have about this is . . . ," "This is important because . . . ," and so on.

A unit of study on information writing in fifth grade would not feel complete without research. The expectation of the Common Core State Standards is that fifth-graders "recall relevant information from experiences or gather relevant information from print and digital sources; summarize or paraphrase information in notes and finished work, and provide a list of sources" (W.5.8). Even though your fifth-graders are writing books on topics of personal expertise, you will absolutely want to channel them to do some quick research, both to double-check facts and to fill in gaps in their knowledge. Teach them that information writers often use research to fact-check or to learn the specialized vocabulary that experts use.

As mentioned earlier, the Common Core State Standards place particular emphasis on domain-specific vocabulary. Perhaps in a mid-workshop teaching point or during your end-of-workshop share session, you could teach your writers that it is not enough to use fancy vocabulary. Nonfiction writers also need to be mindful of different ways to embed definitions of those terms in phrases, sentences, text features, and illustrations. Of course, this is also a good time to remind your writers of the importance of double-checking their spelling, particularly of the fancy vocabulary words they are teaching.

Channel students to think about audience when drafting an introduction and conclusion.

As your writers begin to finish drafting their chapters, it will be helpful to teach them to think always about writing for an audience. The introductions and conclusions in information books often set readers up with additional information and leave them thinking. When writing an introduction, writers can ask, "What do I want to teach readers at the beginning? How can I draw in my reader? How can I give the reader an overview?" Fifth-grade information writers should begin by introducing a topic clearly and providing a general observation and focus, according to the Common Core State Standards (W.5.2a). By fifth grade, writers should be well accustomed to crafting at least basic introductions. They may begin with an interesting quote, fact, or idea and then move into stating the topic and previewing the categories that will follow. Teach your writers to add to these basic introductions by providing not only a topic, but also an angle, or focus, for the topic. For example, a feature article in the January 2008 issue of *Cobblestone* about the Mormon migration in the latter part of the nineteenth century, by Stanley B. Kimball and Gail George Jones, makes clear the authors' angle about this migration right in the introductory paragraph: "They [Mormons] went because religious *persecution* forced them to flee their homes" (p. 8).

When concluding, information writers often sum up the important points, as well as leave readers with something to mull over. According to the Common Core, fifth-graders should "provide a concluding statement or section related to the information or explanation presented" (W.2e). The Reading and Writing Project suggests you have your fifth-graders study the conclusions of mentor texts for ideas on how to structure this section. They may notice that the conclusion in an information text is often structured like a mini-essay, with the writer's opinion followed by some evidence. For example, an article about French bulldogs might end with the following advice to readers: "French bulldogs are a family-friendly, good-natured breed. They do have some health concerns, and they can be stubborn and not so easy to train. These are important things to know if you plan to get one. But if you do decide to take the plunge and get a Frenchie, you won't be disappointed. You will have a loyal companion who is always happy to see you." The introduction and conclusion, then, provide opportunities for the writer to insert some of his or her ideas alongside the information, a skill that will stand them in good stead as they move into middle school.

BEND III: REVISE, FORMAT, AND EDIT TO BEST TEACH READERS

At this point in the unit, your writers will likely have drafted several sections. This is a wonderful time to study their drafts closely, using your Information Writing Checklist, Grade 5 in *Writing Pathways: Performance Assessments and Learning Progressions, Grades K–5*, to assess progress toward the big goals you outlined at the start of the unit to inform your teaching. You may notice, for example, that most of your writers have more or less grouped information correctly into categories, in other words, into topics and subtopics. Notice whether they are being thoughtful about the order in which they present information. Is there a sense that subtopics come in a logical order within sections and that the information within each paragraph is grouped logically? If not, teach them to think of other ways to structure the information within and across sections, perhaps by moving from general information to more specific details or by moving chronologically through the information.

This is also a good time to set up writers to study their own work using the Information Writing Checklist, Grade 5 in *Writing Pathways* and to ask themselves, "Just how good is this information writing that I have done? What are some specific ways I can make my work better?"

In this bend, writers will consider their audience and will think deeply about how their writing sets readers up to be experts. You might begin by teaching your writers to imagine that they are the readers and to reread the text as if for the first time, noticing places where readers might be confused. This is also a wonderful time to set writers up to mentor each other in partnerships, perhaps during the mid-workshop teaching or share. Partners could read each other's work and leave each other Post-its with questions, prompting the owner of the work to further elaborate to answer some of the questions.

Another way that information writers teach is through text features. Just as fifth-grade nonfiction *readers* must use text features to locate information and ultimately boost comprehension (RI.5.5), fifth-grade information *writers* must use text features as a way to help their readers to locate information and to learn more about the topic. Set up your writers to do some inquiry work: studying mentor texts, noticing text features and their purposes. Of course, this work aligns with the work they have been doing in your nonfiction reading workshop. Draw on nonfiction reading charts that support text feature work, and have your writers use these as well as their nonfiction books to mentor themselves as they add text features such as bold words, section headings, embedded and isolated definitions of important terms, illustrations, captions, sidebars, charts, and any other features they may notice. Note that fifth-graders can certainly create their own illustrations and diagrams, or they can use images they find online or in books. However, if they use images from another source, they must credit the source, just as they must credit the source when using a direct quote. You can teach your writers to include a caption with images they use, such as, "Image adapted from thebestwebsiteaboutguidedogs.com."

Remind students to use classroom resources to edit.

You will want to remind writers to draw upon editing strategies you taught earlier. By now your kids will have studied many spelling patterns and high-frequency words through word sorts and a word wall. Certainly you will want to teach kids specifically how to use the word wall when they work on the run during writing time. Never assume that just because the chart or word wall is there, your kids will automatically use it! During the editing phase of this unit, you may want to teach your kids explicitly that when they use the word wall, they will find it helpful if they look at the whole word and take a pretend "photograph" of that word, and then write the *entire* word as best they can without peeking. They should try *not* to copy the word one letter at a time. Words are learned by practicing the whole word. This time of year is also a good time to do a quick informal assessment by looking across kids' independent writing to see which high-frequency words many kids continue to misspell. Even if you already introduced those words as word wall words, you may want to revisit them again and again until most of your children have begun to spell them correctly in their independent writing.

This unit is a good time to teach children to use commas to offset definitions of words in context: "Rings, two circular handlebars hanging on ropes from the ceiling, require a huge amount of upper body strength." In addition, students are ready to investigate the abstract vocabulary that signals agreement (*in addition*, *furthermore*) that compares or contrasts a viewpoint (*however*, *on the other hand*) or that interjects (*or*, *yet*) to advance an idea. You can also draw on the Common Core State Standards for Language and teach the standards that are particularly suited to informational writing. One could certainly imagine CCSS L.5.2d to be particularly important as students learn to integrate sources: "Use underlining, quotation marks, or italics to indicate titles of works." Using punctuation to separate items in a series is another useful punctuation move in information writing (L.5.2a).

BEND IV: BRING WHAT THEY LEARN FROM LONG, INTENSE PROJECTS TO QUICK-WRITES

In this bend, you will teach your writers to channel all they learned over the past weeks into writing quick, focused informational texts. We suggest you begin by taking one class period to give your writers another on-demand assessment using the same prompt that you used at the beginning of the unit. Because this kind of assessment reveals kids' ability to apply the teaching you have done, this, and not necessarily the work your students have done thus far with your support, will be the primary source of information you will use to plan your teaching for this bend. If, for example, you notice that structure is still a challenge for many of your writers, you will want your teaching in this section to be weighted toward planning, helping your writers to remember to divide topics into categories and to group information into these categories. If you notice that your writers aren't developing their pieces with a variety of information, the bulk of your teaching should support elaboration moves.

Information writing gives us a fantastic opportunity to bring the skills we are practicing in literacy into content areas such as science and social studies. In fact, today's session might not even take place during your typical writing workshop block. You might decide to channel your fifth-graders to write some quick informational books during social studies time. Perhaps your students are putting the finishing touches on their feature articles, so the time is right to provide the opportunity to transfer all they have learned to a new experience. When kids do this kind of work, they will move toward higher levels of Norman Webb's Depths of Knowledge (DOK), because they will be using what they learned previously and applying this knowledge to a new task (level 3) and will ultimately be designing their own work process (level 4).

You might begin by teaching your writers to choose a topic that they know well from your current social studies unit. Then, right away, channel them to use what they know about planning for writing to plan quickly, identifying several ways their texts could go, weighing these and choosing one, and then going right on to drafting. Then, in the following session, teach them to study their drafts carefully, using the student-facing checklist you created with them at the start of the unit. You could demonstrate how one might do this work, using a piece of student writing from a previous year. Show writers how you study parts of the draft, checking it against specific points from the checklist. Then, give them a chance to try this with a partner before sending them off to try it with their own drafts.

After your fifth-graders have conducted this self-assessment, they will be ready to make plans for the revision work they will do. This work should be quick and targeted, and your writers should be fairly self-reliant as they identify and execute revisions. Of course, they can be doing some lovely partnership work during this time, sharing their revision plans and the rationale for these plans with each other.

On the third day of this bend, channel your writers to begin yet another quick information text. This time, we find that you can ratchet up the work a notch further by channeling writers to apply all they have learned to a new form of information writing. You could, for example, teach them that information writing is a powerful form of writing that allows writers to create different kinds of texts that convey information. Some of these kinds of texts are speeches, lectures, and brochures. Writers might choose different forms at different times, depending on the audience they want to teach, but the principles of good information writing always stay the same. On this day, show writers some samples of these kinds of texts. You might, for example, show a YouTube video with a child giving a mini-lecture. There are many choices: one we've enjoyed recently features a five-year-old girl named Madison teaching about makeup application. You can also show a fifth-grader's student council speech, of which there are many on YouTube, as a mentor for speech writing. As your writers plan, draft, and revise these new pieces with more independence than ever before, remind them that that they can use their own writing as a mentor text. Your writers can pull out the information books they have been working on in writing workshop that are nearly publishing-ready and can mine these for good information writing moves that they can transfer to their new texts.

A FINAL CELEBRATION: USE WHAT WE KNOW ABOUT NONFICTION WRITING TO TEACH YOUNGER STUDENTS HOW TO WRITE THEIR OWN

For a final celebration, choose a younger class that has not yet studied information writing. This class could be a class you already have a relationship with, or they could be a class that you just borrow for a day.

Give your students time to rehearse, with you listening in and giving teaching pointers. Some students might want to include a ton of charts and other flashy things. You will likely want your students to keep the props to a minimum. The simpler their teaching, the more easily it will be executed and the more likely it will be that the younger students pick up a few ideas they can try in their own writing. Remind students that they should pick just a couple of things they think are the most important for the younger writers to learn and to be sure to repeat those two things as often as possible. If students are having a hard time prioritizing, suggest they start by thinking about structure and elaboration.

You might organize the celebration so that your fifth-graders teach in shifts. This will help keep the volume and energy levels optimal and also will provide your class with an opportunity to observe each other. After the celebration, you may want to convene your writers in the meeting area, giving them a chance to bask in the feelings of collegiality teachers often have after a job well done. Then, guide them to reflect on what they have learned about information writing and what they will carry with them after the close of the unit.

Information Writing
Reading, Research, and Writing in the Content Areas

RATIONALE/INTRODUCTION

If you imagine a writing unit of study in which students are engaged in research projects, chances are good that the unit that comes to mind will be very much like this one. This unit is built around the assumption that students are studying a social studies topic during at least one other time in the day—during either reading, social studies, or both. Within the writing workshop, students proceed through the process, starting with collecting notes, then writing-to-learn, and then writing research reports under the influence of mentor texts, culminating in prepublication work. The unit provides you with generic tools that will be effective with any topic. You may want to teach it before *The Lens of History: Research Reports*, although students will benefit from it after as well. Either way, this unit, in tandem with *The Lens of History*, will give children the opportunity to practice the information writing standards called for in the fifth-grade Common Core State Standards.

MANDATES, TESTS, STANDARDS

This is a fairly traditional unit, designed to support basic skills in writing research reports. More specifically, the unit gives students an opportunity to use writing to teach others about what they learn in the content area. This research report helps meet all the writing demands for the CCSS' informational standards. These writing standards require students to construct informative or explanatory texts that examine a topic and convey ideas and information clearly, grouping related information into paragraphs and sections that will be formatted with headings and subheadings. When writing these texts, students are expected to develop the topic with facts, definitions, concrete details, quotations, or examples. Students can link ideas within categories of information using words and phrases, such as *another*, *for example*, and *because*. The use of precise language or content-specific vocabulary is required, as well as providing a concluding statement or section.

A SUMMARY OF THE BENDS IN THE ROAD FOR THIS UNIT

In Bend I (Write to Develop Expertise and Grow Ideas), students will learn to capture what they are learning, thinking, and writing to grow their ideas. They will look at pictures and other information and write observations, descriptions, labels, and captions. You will also teach students note-taking strategies, such as boxes and bullets. Students will learn to synthesize information and ideas quickly as they read and write.

In Bend II (Write to Develop a Research Base of Knowledge and Deepen Our Expertise in a Topic), students' research will focus on content areas through reading, informational videos, field trips, and so on. Students will narrow down their topics and then expand their knowledge about that chosen topic, coming up with questions and hypotheses to guide their own research. They will then reflect upon, organize, and prioritize their research and notes.

In Bend III (Study Mentors and Write Drafts of Research Reports), students will begin drafting their research reports, relying on your work, mentor authors, and other sources to see how these should go. Students will organize their work into chapters and subtopics, working to see what organizing strategy (compare/contrast, cause/effect, and so on) best fits their material. Students will elaborate with more detailed information, vocabulary words and definitions, or drawings and diagrams. You could also have your students pair up with writing partners for additional feedback.

In Bend IV (Revise, Edit, and Publish to Get Ready to Teach Others), students will choose their best work to include in their research report. Then they will revise and edit this work. Revisions could include adding new subheadings, drawings, or text features into the piece, as well as considering their own "slant" or perspective. The celebration might involve staging a research symposium or acting out scenes.

GETTING READY

The social studies content you choose for this month should be highly engaging. You'll want to choose a topic for which you have many resources: books, videos, primary documents. You'll want to be sure that your whole class can study many subtopics within the main topic, so you'll want to ask yourself, "Does this topic have *breadth*?" Instead of doing a month-long study of just the battles of the American Revolution, for example, you'll likely want to broaden the topic. This way, children could also study the dress of the time period and what life was like for those who were not fighting. They could compare different kinds of colonies, events leading up to the Revolutionary War, leadership during the time, and so on.

This month, it's essential that you immerse your students in nonfiction, for children can only write about new learning if they've truly learned something new. Flood your children with images, facts, and stories about the time period of study a week or two *before* launching this writing unit so they'll begin on Day One with lots and lots to say. As your researchers become knowledgeable, they'll be eager to share what they've learned and the ideas they have about all the new information they've acquired. Students will, then, begin to turn their research into a writing project, or you can imagine small-group or class-wide projects.

You will want to consider the following questions.

- What's the topic of study? What will my whole class be learning about? What are the choices for students within that larger topic?

- What materials do I have and need that can serve as writing mentors, and what do I have that I can use to teach the content?

- When will I begin this unit to ensure that children know enough about the content before they write about it?

- Will my students be working in partners, small groups, or independently to create their final pieces?

BEND I: WRITE TO DEVELOP EXPERTISE AND GROW IDEAS

Your job in the weeks leading up to the launch of this writing unit, and in the first week or two of the unit, will be to teach your children a lot about the topic of study. You might want to set up a special place for this collection of information, sketching, and writing to be housed. Perhaps it's a social studies folder that they decorate with a picture of themselves as a historian or person of the time period on the cover. Perhaps it's just a tabbed section in their already-established social studies notebook or writer's notebook.

Decide if you want children forming groups around one topic of inquiry or whether you want children to each survey the whole topic, gaining broad knowledge, before zeroing-in on one to study with more depth. For example, if you are choosing to study the colonial period as a whole-class topic, you might steer the class into groups that study subtopics. You could offer ideas for subtopics that are guided by your content standards—for example, life in the colonies; comparing New England, the Middle and Southern Colonies, and Europe. You could also think about the social studies thematic strands and have children choose one of those: culture; time, continuity, and change; people, places, and environments; individual development and identity; individuals, groups, and institutions; power, authority, and governance; production, distribution, and consumption; science, technology, and society; global connections; civic ideas and responsibility. It could also be that children individually choose their own subtopics that they derive from reading and thinking broadly during writing workshop. Whichever way you choose, this compartmentalization of topics and subtopics helps students see the relationship between two or more ideas or concepts in a historical context (which the Common Core State Standards refer to in the "key ideas and details" standard).

Immerse writers in nonfiction texts.

Before the unit begins, you will have gathered all sorts of nonfiction materials—expository nonfiction, narrative nonfiction, maps, primary documents, digital texts, and even images. Your students will be engaged in partnerships or clubs reading about this content. They'll have time to talk to one another to deepen their understanding and grow ideas. They'll mark interesting parts of the book with thoughts and reactions, ready to share with friends. As readers, they will also be able to read and understand a wider array of nonfiction books: narrative nonfiction that takes the reader through a timeline of historical events, expository nonfiction (information and all-about) that teaches all about a topic, and question-and-answer books that invite the reader to wonder alongside the author. The writing inside these books and texts will serve as writing mentors, providing writers with a wealth of mentoring opportunities around authorial choices, craft moves, and publishing possibilities.

In addition to reading these texts to learn content, students will read as researchers, with the specific intent to gather important information and parlay it into their own research reports. These reports are similar to information books in that they present information about a topic of expertise. They are different, though, because research reports present information in a format that is more reminiscent of an essay structure, rather than a book format. Research reports contain information separated into sections, potentially with headings, and have diagrams or text boxes containing supplemental information. Some of you may envision your students using publishing software, such as Microsoft Publisher, to create visually compelling reports. It might also be the case that some of you may feel students need another round of informational book writing and might choose to design this unit around another exposure to that form of publication.

Demonstrate how writers capture new learning in notebooks to grow ideas.

As the unit begins, you will immerse your children in all the different ways that they can write about what they are learning in the reading or content area workshop. You will want to teach them that social scientists write in many ways for many purposes. During this first week of the unit, their purpose for writing will be to capture what they are learning, thinking, and writing to grow their ideas. Therefore, you will probably teach them that their notebooks are collections of many kinds of writing.

One kind of writing is observational writing. They will record in extreme detail all that they observe while studying a primary document or drawing from the time period through observations and sketches. During writing workshop, you will teach how they can go back to those sketches and observations and write in words, phrases, sentences, and even paragraphs about what they have seen and sketched. Teach them that they can use prompts like "I notice . . . ," "I see . . . ," and "This reminds me of . . . " One way to ensure your children are doing this writing in as much detail as possible is to teach them to remember the thinking skills of a social scientist: considering cause and effect, comparing and contrasting, evaluating, drawing inferences. When social scientists write observations, they want their readers to be able to picture what they are writing about, so they try to write about every little tiny thing they see, using the most precise words they possibly can. They also add what it feels like, right down to the smallest detail.

Another kind of writing is sketching with labels and captions. While reading nonfiction texts, students may have drawn a striking image from one of their books and then labeled it using precise vocabulary. In writing workshop, they could add captions that explain the image in greater detail. It is conceivable that some students feeling full of the energy and enthusiasm of discovery will add a few words to one sketch and then move on to another and another. Therefore, it is important to teach them that historians (and writers!) linger. This means teaching them to add all that they can add to their sketches, in both words and images.

You may also want to teach children some strategies for note-taking. They may learn to take notes as boxes and bullets, recording a main idea and supporting facts. You may teach them to read a chunk of text and think, "What is the most important part of this? What facts support that important part?" You may teach them to keep their topic of inquiry in mind, if they have decided on one at this point, and return to their book for notes. That is, they'll be using tables of contents and an index to find sections in a text to reread and take notes on what they're rereading. All the while, they'll take notes on cards, Post-its, or small pieces of paper that can later be sorted and organized. The size of the piece of paper or card will help to ensure that they aren't copying sections from the book, but instead are jotting quick notes about what they've learned.

If social scientists simply put their diagrams and observations into the book without any other writing, the people reading the books would probably be left wondering, "What does this mean? What does the writer think about all this stuff?" Teach students to help their future readers by writing their ideas that accompany the research they've begun to collect in their notebooks. Teach students to develop their ideas by asking themselves, "What do I think about this?" or "What is important about this?" and then writing it down. That way, when someone reads their writing they won't be left wondering, "What does this mean?"

Social scientists may write an annotated timeline. They take notes about events that happened in sequence. On the top of the timeline, they might record facts about what happened and the date it happened. Below, they might annotate this timeline with their own thoughts or ideas. You can imagine the student making a map of Harriet Tubman's journeys in her notebook or a map of the main paths of the Underground Railroad and Harriet's stops on it. Or a timeline of her escapes. Or even a quick sketch of the plantation from which she escaped. The main point of this kind of writing is that it is quick, and its purpose is to synthesize information and ideas as you read, to get ready to write.

BEND II: WRITE TO DEVELOP A RESEARCH BASE OF KNOWLEDGE AND DEEPEN OUR EXPERTISE IN A TOPIC

All of the reading and research in nonfiction is the fuel for what children write in writing workshop. At this point in the unit, students will most likely be breaking up into different category or subtopic groups, taking on a specific angle of your whole-class study. The experience of the whole-class research community in the previous bend will support students' independence in smaller research groups. These smaller research groups help meet the demands of the Common Core State Standards' speaking and listening standards, which ask students to engage effectively in a range of collaborative discussions with diverse partners, building on others' ideas and expressing their own clearly. During these conversations, students will come to discussions prepared, having read materials they can explicitly draw on as they explore the ideas under discussion. It will be helpful for students to write in their special notebooks or folders, collecting their thoughts, questions, and ideas to bring to their group. Smokey Daniels describes some of this in *Subjects Matter*, which may be a helpful resource for you. He encourages students to trade notebooks once a week and write to each other in their notebooks, responding to each other's research, reflections, and ideas. As a whole class across these next weeks, your children will continue to listen to read-alouds, watch videos, and even take field trips.

Inspire writers to expand learning by writing notes, observations, and questions.

In this second bend, while students are reading to learn about more specific parts of their topics, they will be using writing to expand their content area knowledge. They'll write longer about initial notes and observations they made, question new knowledge they've learned, or generate new ideas. Students will need to begin to fuel their own research. One way to do this is to generate questions and pursue a line of thinking. Questions that begin with *what* or *when* lead researchers to quick answers that clarify information. Questions that begin with *why* or *how* lead researchers on longer pursuits to answer the questions. For instance, initially students might ask, "When did the Underground Railroad begin?" and move on to question "How did slaves learn the safe codes to use while traveling toward freedom?"

Additionally, historians often use their notebooks to question and wonder. Because it is important that children continue to write with volume and stamina, you will also want to teach them to try to hypothesize answers to these musings. You could imagine kids saying things like "I wonder why . . . " or "How come . . . " Teach kids to catch these thoughts by quickly jotting them in their notebooks. Then, teach them to think through possible answers by using prompts such as "Maybe . . . ," "Could it be . . . ," "But what about . . . ," and "The best explanation is . . . " For example, a child might look at a picture in a book about Colonial America. The picture shows a woman raking or hoeing in the field. Two other females—another adult and a child—are in the background on their knees, also tending to crops. The caption reads, "Everyone in the family pitched in to help with the chores." The child might write in her notebook:

> I notice in the picture that there are three women working in the field. It looks like the field is right next to their house. It makes me think this is their own private garden. It's not very big; it might be that the food that they grow there is just for them and their family. The caption says that the whole family pitches in to help with the chores. But I only see girls and women in the picture. It could be that the women and girls had different chores than the men had. I'm surprised that a woman's chore would be tending to the garden, though. From what I already knew, I think of their chores as being things like sewing and cooking. I'll be interested to learn more about that.

Guide students as they capture thoughts and realizations about new learning.

As the unit progresses, you will notice that your children are beginning to have more developed thoughts, ideas, and opinions about the class study. Congratulate your students on figuring out the value of writing to think about their topic. Here you might want to teach kids that historians not only write about what they observe, but they also write about what they think about these observations. Therefore, you might teach kids to look back over the writing they've collected in their notebooks and to write long about what they are thinking or realizing. These entries might begin with "I know some things about . . . " and continue with examples: "One thing I know . . . Another thing I know . . . " This could then lead into some writing to think: "This makes me realize . . . ," "This helps me understand . . . " Or "I used to think . . . But, now I know . . . My thinking changed because . . . "

This is a good time to either remind or teach students to make their own graphic organizers and develop their own systems for jotting as they read. They'll probably begin by putting Post-its on the texts they are reading. Then they can turn to their notebooks, and this is a good time to review the boxes-and-bullets structure of:

- Idea
- Example
- Example
- Example

Some of the students' books will naturally be organized like this as ideas and examples, and they can use the headings and subheadings to guide their note-taking. Often, however, they'll need to read over the text, think about the idea they have about this section, and then organize their notes with their original ideas and examples that they carefully selected from the text. Later these will make good ordinate and subordinate sections for their research report. You may also teach your students to write full sentences and paragraphs in their notebooks, structured along the same lines as the boxes and bullets—almost like mini-essays, with an idea and evidence and perhaps some reflection. For instance, you can model writing a notebook entry that sounds like:

I think Harriet Tubman is amazing because she was so brave. For instance, they tracked her with dogs and teams of men who wanted to capture her. They would track her for miles and miles and she had to walk in streams, and run at night. She was also brave because they did capture her, and she always escaped again. I can hardly imagine being caught, and then waiting for the moment to sneak out again.

Teach your students to write reflections, in which they look over their notes and write entries describing their new understandings and their emotions about what they learn: what they find upsetting, what they admire, and so on. This is where they will be developing their own ideas about what they read and putting those ideas into lots of words. Teach them to use the sentence starters you used for essays earlier in the year, such as "Some people think . . . but I think . . . ," "In other words . . . ," "Another way to say this is . . . ," and so on.

Help students organize and prioritize new information.

You may see some of your students struggling to use accurate research practices about what to cite and reference in their writing. Some students struggle to determine what information is important to note and write down for later use. Teach students the strategy of looking across their notes and listing, for example, the three most important parts about what they are studying. For instance, if students have been reading about the Underground Railroad, they might say that Harriet Tubman, the struggles the slaves faced, and the new opportunities awaiting them were three important parts. Then, teach students to use these categories as filters, using them as guides for gathering important research. Some teachers find it helpful to put these three or more categories on index cards so that children can reread texts or their notes using the index cards like bookmarks, stopping to copy important information on them.

You'll also want to teach students to prioritize the research they gather, determining which research is most important to include. You might take this opportunity to remind students of the ranking strategy work they learned earlier in the year. Remind them that using -er words (*bigger, lesser, greater, smaller*) is a helpful way to determine importance and prioritize information. Imagine students working with their research clubs, holding lists of facts and examples, asking each other, "Which had the *larger* effect?" "What had the *lesser* impact on . . . " "Who had the *greater* influence on . . . " Other key words, such as *most* or *least*, are helpful to incorporate into conversations or writing when prioritizing information. Students can use phrases such as "*most* influential" or "*least* effective" to sift through research and make decisions on which points to refer to in their later writing.

Demonstrate how to use your own words to record new learning.

You'll want to seize this opportunity to teach children to cite research correctly, showing them how to incorporate research and put it in their own words. When practicing paraphrasing, you might find it helpful for students to write the research fact on one side of an index card and then rewrite it on the other side of the card from memory. Or perhaps you'll use the structure of the research club and have students play a written form of "telephone." One student might write a research example they want to paraphrase at the top of his or her notebook and pass it around to other members of the club, where each student reworks the example by replacing verbs, adding descriptive words or phrases, or otherwise reworking the sentence. Of course, you'll teach into preserving the accuracy of the information. For instance, you might model reworking the research example:

> Harriet Tubman is perhaps the most well known of all the Underground Railroad's "conductors."
> During a ten-year span she made 19 trips into the South and escorted over 300 slaves to freedom.

into

> Harriet Tubman is maybe the most famous of all the Underground Railroad's guides. Over ten
> years, Tubman traveled 19 times into the South to accompany more than 300 slaves to freedom.

BEND III: STUDY MENTORS AND WRITE DRAFTS OF RESEARCH REPORTS

This third bend is the intensive writing portion of the unit, where students pore over the notes they've taken and figure out ways to piece together different aspects of their reports. Students will be looking closely at mentors and writing many potential parts of their reports on an aspect of the whole-class study.

Students will need mentors as they draft their research reports. At first, it might feel as though you have little to no samples available for your students, especially as you probably don't have a bin in your library labeled "Research Reports!" First, you'll have your own demonstration writing. Second, you can access sites like *TIME for Kids* for sample articles or reports. Lastly, the nonfiction and content area books that line the shelves of your libraries include incredibly rich and valuable samples of writing that students can use as mentors. Just think of the pages that include lots of information categorized with headings, tables, or text boxes. Your goal is to collect many texts that can serve as models for what your children will make, not to collect all books about the topic of study. You might even give writers mentor texts about topics that are very different from what your children will write about so that they cannot copy the content but instead are inspired by the layout, structure, and craft of the books.

Teach students to organize nonfiction information into chapters.

Remind your students of their learning from the year: often expository nonfiction is divided up into chapters, each with its own subtopic. To make a research report like this, the writer probably learned a lot about the topic, collecting facts and ideas, and then organized those ideas into categories. Or instead, the writer might have learned a lot about the topic, thought of categories, and then searched for specific facts to fit into those categories. You might also draw from some work students have done writing about nonfiction, showing them how some sections take on a compare-and-contrast format and others, a cause-and-effect format. You'll help your children to see that nonfiction is detailed with specific words about the topic and partner sentences that explain, define, and teach the reader.

It is very important to read aloud and to do shared reading and shared writing of nonfiction. Reading like a writer and writing as a whole class will serve as students' immersion in what they'll write and will serve as a reminder of how to use mentors. For example, you could make an overhead of two sections from a nonfiction text or place them on your Smart Board and have the whole class read the pages together. You could ask your children questions, leading them to notice aspects of how the parts are structured and about the kinds of information they find. You could ask them to talk about how they think a writer might have made this particular page, with this particular kind of writing. All the while, you can be making charts that serve as "directions" for how to make the different sections that will form their research reports. A chart could have a Xerox of a page with arrows labeling the different parts or sections. Then, during shared writing you may show your children how to use the resources, including mentor texts and charts, to make that kind of writing.

All the while you'll also remind students that their notebooks are valuable resources filled with their thoughts, questions, observations, and conclusions. They could look back at what they've already written and use it not only as inspiration, but also for elaboration. Or they could take detailed drawings or diagrams that they created in their notebooks and cut them out and tape them to new pages, adding lines of text on the bottom of the page. You might teach children to look back to their detailed drawings to write more on the page. Or teach them to go back to a sentence where they wrote a vocabulary word that might be new for their readers and try to write another sentence to support it, defining what it means. Other children would benefit from thinking about how to elaborate on other parts of pages, such as the captions or labels. To decide what to teach in these few days, it would be helpful to look at your children's writing to see what they are already doing and teach them some new ways to elaborate.

Writing partners will help students move toward more independence and away from depending on you for content and writing feedback. You might teach a lesson about how to utilize a writing partner to give ideas for what information would be helpful to include. You can teach your children how to use their partners as sounding boards, asking them, "Did that make sense?" or "Do you feel like there is anything missing?" or "What questions do you still have about my topic after you read that page?" Later, you might ask children to read each other's work, making sure what they've written makes sense.

If you find that some of your children are including more information on each section than fits their topics, you might teach them to read back over what they have, making sure to stay focused on what the sections are about.

BEND IV: REVISE, EDIT, AND PUBLISH TO GET READY TO TEACH OTHERS

At this point in the unit, many of your children have drafted many sections in a variety of structures. In this final week, you will want to rally their passion and purpose in studying history toward sharing what they have learned with others. First, you will teach them to lay out all the writing they have done and choose the best parts to turn into a research report. They'll take those pieces and will revise, edit, and publish to share at the celebration. You might teach them to choose by thinking about their audience and asking, "Would others be interested in reading about . . . ?" Then, you will teach them to return to their mentors, reading closely to notice the details and subtlety within a given structure. You will definitely want to help kids notice and then try revision techniques again—things like partner sentences (if you can write one sentence about something, you can write two or more), sequencing (going from the main idea to supporting details), vocabulary (using the specific words that match the class study), and adding extra sections of charts (diagrams, timelines, captions, front covers, back covers, and blurbs). It's okay, and probable, that you will be reteaching some of the same lessons you taught earlier.

Channel students to revise and edit informational texts for clarity.

Since these are informational texts that children have authored this month, you might remind them to check that their paragraphs each have a clear topic sentence and that the boxes-and-bullets structure is clear to the reader. Model how you might split one paragraph into two smaller paragraphs to make each present a distinct idea. Ask writers to revise their headings and subheadings. Urge them to ponder, "Would a new subheading help the reader understand this part of the text more fully? Would a table of contents benefit the reader?" You'll also want to alert writers to the diagrams they might have included in the text. Ask them to revise these diagrams, looking them over carefully to ensure there are adequate captions and labels that explain each diagram clearly to the reader. "Does the diagram explain or connect to the text on that page?" children might ask themselves. "Would this diagram work better for another portion of the text? Should I shift it there?"

Part of the revision process might include inserting new text features to give more clarity to the writing. Suggest that writers insert a text box or two if their readers might benefit from knowing an extra fact. Demonstrate how one might choose a title and a cover illustration for one's research report. Before they begin their final edits for spelling and punctuation, ask writers to think, "Is this report teaching the reader about my topic in a clear way? What can I do to make my teaching even clearer?" Guide students to revise for focus or cohesion. The various parts of the report should not feel disjointed. Instead they should blend together or build on each other.

Writers might consider if they want their piece to have a slant, or angle, or if they might include their own or others' perspectives on just one part, such as the introduction. Using what they know about analytical writing from previous units, they might return to some of the informational writing and elaborate by providing perspective.

As the unit draws to a close, it will be important to remind your young historians that they've already learned so much about how to fix up their writing for publication—capitalization, beginning and ending punctuation, and limiting the number of *and*s in any given sentence. You can teach kids to edit their work by rereading it to make sure it all makes sense, crossing out and adding parts as necessary. Kids can check their writing for frequently misspelled words and spelling patterns they have been working on, all by themselves.

Finally, to fancy up the pieces for publishing, kids might use photographs just like many informational texts. They might also add more details to their pictures and diagrams, as well as color. Kids might also make important vocabulary bold or underlined.

Some teachers may prefer for students to share their new understandings in projects. This can include acting out important scenes (narrating why this moment is important in American history), having a symposium on the issues of the Revolution and formation of government that still affect us today, using film, picture books, and articles to compare the American Revolution to others that have happened around the world, and so on.

Literary and Comparative Essays

RATIONALE/INTRODUCTION

By this point in the year, you likely have amassed a lot of data on your students' abilities to write to support opinions and arguments. If you conducted a summative assessment following your previous unit, you can consider that data now and study patterns and trends you are noticing across the class. You might also discuss your observations with your grade colleagues, together considering patterns of need across the grade. Because you have planned your assessments in conjunction across the year and have gathered consistent data, that data can be compared, and you can engage in problem solving and planning together. You will want to use this unit, like all units, to teach with urgency to support all writers in meeting and exceeding grade-level expectations. If there are writers across the grade who are showing difficulty in making progress, this is a time to blow the whistle and gather all stakeholders together. Your grade team might brainstorm ways to work together to help those writers who most need extra support. Perhaps one day a week after school, each member of the grade will teach a small group consisting of students from across the grade. Perhaps you will decide to modify writing homework. You will want to adapt your teaching to meet the needs of your students, but you will also want to constantly keep your eye on the grade-level expectations you are working to help your students to meet and exceed. You will want to have writers bring out their goals and action plans as well as the Opinion Writing Checklist you created as a class during the previous units and revise action plans, setting specific steps for how to reach goals. You will want to ensure that writers have a deep understanding of their strengths and needs so that they can continue to be invested, responsible partners in their own learning.

If you did not conduct a summative assessment after the previous unit, you will want to gather current data. To do so, you may decide to administer opinion writing on demand. You can see previous opinion writing units for support in how to administer and assess on-demand assessments, and as always, the Opinion Writing Checklist, Grade 5 is available in the book *Writing Pathways: Performance Assessments and Learning Progressions, Grades K–5*. This checklist offers support in deciding next teaching steps, providing informative feedback, and helping students to gain a crystal-clear sense of the expectations toward which they are working.

Just as writing allows us to pause in the hurry of our lives to really notice, experience, and reflect, so too, can writing give us a tool to pause in our hurried reading to really pay attention to characters and ideas in our books. This unit aims to make reading a more intense, thoughtful experience for children, equipping them with tools they need to write expository essays that advance an idea about a piece of literature. This unit relies upon children's prior experience writing interpretive essays, suggesting they do similar work. In *Shaping Texts: From Essay and Narrative to Memoir*, students were offered the chance to write about connections between texts and themselves, and some tried their hand at writing essays interpreting characters. Many teachers have found that students need repeated practice at this work, and this unit aims to provide that and raise the level of their work in writing arguments about texts. Students will move from exploring an idea about one piece of literature to comparing and contrasting that idea across two pieces of literature, which is to say, this unit of study is twofold. Students will first learn to craft literary essays about one text and then bring in a second text to craft a comparative literary essay or to inform their thinking about the first text with the help of another text. Many teachers decide to pair this writing unit with a reading unit in which students are organized into book clubs, reading sets of texts that go together in some way and thinking interpretively about the lessons or themes inherent in these texts.

By this point in the year, students have likely had ample opportunity to engage in work that sets them up to meet the Common Core's expectations for fifth-graders' opinion writing. One of the major demands of these standards is that students be "logical" in their writing. Fifth-graders are expected to "logically group ideas" (W.5.1) and "provide logically ordered reasons" (W.5.1b). Thus, it is crucial this year that students understand why they are structuring their essays in particular ways and that they make intentional choices about how to organize their work. Fifth-graders are also expected to write arguments about topics *and texts*. This expectation is the first Anchor Standard for College and Career Readiness. This unit is designed to strengthen and hone students' essay-writing skills. It is designed to be taught following "The Personal and Persuasive Essay" unit outlined earlier in this book and either before or after *The Research-Based Argument Essay* unit. This unit will support your writers in transferring and applying all that they have learned to now write arguments about texts.

Meanwhile, this unit will offer you a chance to teach into and shore up weaker areas in your students' argument writing. You will want to have all of your data from across the year in hand to ensure that you are helping students move along a trajectory of work and make progress in large, visible ways. Then, too, this unit will prepare your students for the demands of writing quick, well-structured essays grounded in textual evidence should they encounter this kind of writing on a standardized test.

A SUMMARY OF THE BENDS IN THE ROAD FOR THIS UNIT

In each of the chock-full units in this bend, your writers will cycle through the writing process. First, they will tackle a literary essay about one text; next, they will try their hands at comparative essays in which they explore two texts; and finally, they will choose one essay to edit and publish.

In Bend I (Writing Literary Essays about Texts), your students will write literary essays using short texts. You will channel your writers through the process of essay writing, beginning with collecting some ideas about themes of texts by reading closely and doing some thinking on the page in their notebooks. After a few days, you will guide your writers in developing thesis statements and supports for their essays, and then, you will channel them to find evidence that supports the structures they have chosen. As your writers draft, you will remind them of all they know about structure and elaboration in argument writing.

Before the second bend starts, you might have your students write quick essays, taking no more than ten to twelve minutes, as a way to help them to transfer and apply all they have learned and to do some self-assessment using the Opinion Writing Checklist.

In Bend II (Write across Texts), you will push students to make more complex interpretations of texts as they write comparative essays using a second text. They will study a theme and its development across two texts.

In Bend IV (Edit and Publish: Prepare Essays to Share with the World), your writers will choose one essay to edit and publish and then will celebrate the work they have done, perhaps publishing their final work digitally on a book review site so that other readers may learn from their interpretations.

GETTING READY
Gather Materials for Students

Of course, this is a unit that is very much dependent upon students having access to meaningful texts. These texts need not necessarily be whole novels. In fact, this unit will likely go more smoothly if students are writing about short texts, ideally texts that you and your class have studied throughout the year. There is nothing to be gained from the texts being unfamiliar ones. If you are running a concurrent reading workshop in which students are thinking interpretively about texts, then by all means, they can write about these texts during writing workshop. If not, that is all the more reason to choose short and familiar texts. Gather these texts and create a packet for each student.

A note about difficulty: be sure that you include texts that are calibrated to the level at which each reader can read, with over 96% fluency, accuracy, and comprehension. We encourage you to provide stories that are rich, complex, and well crafted enough that they reward close study. Cynthia Rylant's book *Every Living Thing* has some wonderful examples of short stories. Eve Bunting's and Patricia Palacco's picture books are also very meaty. Many of the short stories in Gary Soto's anthology *Baseball in April* are excellent; we are particularly fond of "The Marble Champ." Sandra Cisneros's *House on Mango Street* is another lovely collection of powerful short stories.

Anticipate the Trajectory of Students' Work across the Unit

You will need to decide from the outset how much time you are going to spend in each part of the unit. For example, if you know that your students have studied literary essays focusing on a single text, you may only want to spend two weeks working on the first essay. This allows for more time to consider, draft, and revise the comparative essay. If you want to spend more time honing the single-text essay, you may spend only a week in the comparative work. However, this may not be enough time to take the essay all the way through the publishing process. A third option would be to develop a single-text and comparative essay through the drafting stage, then have students choose which essay to revise, edit, and publish. If you are not moving from this unit into a test prep unit, you may choose to have students end the unit by taking a day to quickly write a literary essay. If you'll be working on that during test prep, then you needn't include it in this unit. This work would support the kind of writing that students are often asked to do on tests and in school now and throughout college. The last bend could then be a revision bend in which the writers go back to all previous drafts and revise them.

BEND I: WRITING LITERARY ESSAYS ABOUT TEXTS

Encourage students to collect ideas and then choose a seed idea.

As suggested above, it will be helpful if you gather a collection of short texts that are familiar to your students or that most of them can read with a high level of accuracy. On each of the first few days of the unit, demonstrate a different strategy writers might use to grow deeper ideas about texts. You might start by simply teaching that just as essayists scrutinize the details of their lives for ideas, literary essayists scrutinize texts for ideas, reading with rapt attentiveness and then capturing their thinking in notebooks.

You might also teach that writers aim to capture an image that stayed with them after finishing a story, writing about why that image feels so unforgettable and exploring how the image fits with the whole story.

To help your fifth-graders linger with the beauty of the language of a text, you might teach them that writers sometimes copy a line or two of text onto a page of a notebook and then write to explore why they found that line so powerful and how that part fits with the whole story. You might also teach writers that it can pay off to record a turning point in the book, again exploring how this moment fits with the whole book. Finally, you might teach that writers can also explore ideas by writing about how they might live differently if they took the lessons in the story really seriously.

Of course, you will not want to suggest and demonstrate a strategy and then expect every writer to use it to explore the same text at the same time. Instead, you will want writers to draw from the toolkit of possible strategies. Emphasize to students the value of rereading and reconsidering texts, allowing for new thinking with each subsequent read. Whatever strategies students choose to use, the goal of this part of the unit is the same: looking closely at texts to *really* read, reread, revisit, and reconsider all of their details and nuances, and to capture some new ideas in their notebooks.

After a day or two of collecting, guide your writers to select one text to write about for the remainder of the bend. Next, channel children to select bits of the writing they have done about this text that seem especially important and to begin to elaborate on those ideas. Writers can look closely at the text they've selected and write about aspects of that text that stand out, writing "I notice . . . " and then recording their observations about the text. Encourage them to write long about this, extending their observation by drawing on thought prompts such as "The surprising thing about this is . . . " or "The important thing about this is . . . " or "The thought this gives me is . . . " or "I wonder if . . . "

Next, teach your students that literary essayists know ahead of time that some places are rich ground for literary analysis. You might teach this as an inquiry lesson to place a higher cognitive demand on your writers and ask them to investigate what places in a text seem most worthy of pausing over to look for ideas. You can gather their ideas to co-construct a class chart. If students do not mention certain types of moments, you might help them to notice some of the kinds of moments that are often entry points to great thinking, such as moments of character change, the lessons that characters learn, and the issues (personal or social) that the characters face.

At this point in the unit, it may be helpful to remind children of their work in the interpretive essay unit, when they observed their lives and created "thought patches" in their notebooks by writing, "The thought I have about this is . . . " or "This makes me realize that . . . " If students are not applying this work, you might teach them to see that in this unit, they can pause as they read to observe what is happening to a character and then grow an idea using the same sentence starters. You can teach children that these thought patches can be extended and that they can use thought prompts to grow their thinking. Be aware that children are apt to extend their thinking by providing examples only, and you will want to help them to linger with their ideas, too. Teach them to record an idea using new words by saying, "That is . . . " or "In other words . . . " and then rephrasing the idea. Teach them to entertain possibilities by writing, "Could it be that . . . ," "Perhaps . . . ," or "Some may say that . . . " Phrases such as "Furthermore . . . ," "This connects with . . . ," "On the other hand . . . ," "But you might ask . . . ," "This is true because . . . ," or "I am realizing that . . . " can also keep children elaborating upon their ideas. If you hope that children will write literary essays in which they articulate the lessons they believe a character learns in a story or essays that name the theme or idea a text teaches, then it will be important for you to provide children with strategies for growing these sorts of ideas in particular.

Teach students to write thesis statements and plan boxes and bullets.

After children have collected responses to reading in their writer's notebooks, remind them that they already know how to reread a notebook to find seed ideas. In the interpretive essay unit, students will have literally found seed *ideas*, and they'll need to do something similar to that exercise now. Remind your writers to push for seed ideas that are central to a text and provocative. If they need support, there are a few templates that seem to especially work for literary essays. Help writers to use these with elasticity so they are still able to write about the ideas that matter most to them. Some writers will have a claim about a character or a text and then give reasons for that claim, as they did in their interpretive essays. "So and so is a good friend because A, because B, and above all because C." Or "So and so succeeds because of A, B, and above all, because of C." Or "This is about so and so who learns/turns out to be/changes to be/ becomes [what, by the end]. Early in the text [in contrast] . . . Later in the text . . . "

For example, "*Because of Winn-Dixie* is the story of a lonely girl, Opal, who learns that she isn't alone after all. In the beginning of the story, she is lonely, and by the end, the whole town has become peopled with people she cares about." Or "'Spaghetti' is the story of a lonely boy, Gabriel, who learns to open himself to love. At the beginning of the story . . . "

There is another template that often works well for literary essays. Earlier, in the interpretive essay unit, we suggested that sometimes writers may want to write journey-of-thought essays, and these often begin, "At first I thought . . . but now I realize . . . " Students may write, "When I first read . . . I thought it was about [the external plot-driven story], but now, rereading it, I realize it is about [the internal story]." Or "Some people think . . . is about [the external plot], but I think that it is really about [the deeper meaning]." This thesis would lead a writer to first write about the plot, the external story, and then write about the theme, or the under-story.

Other students may want to write a thesis statement that follows a different structure: "My feelings about . . . are complicated. On the one hand, I think . . . On the other hand, I think . . . " In this structure, students can explore how their feelings or ideas about a story, character, or theme are conflicted; the reader feels more than one thing at the same time. "My feelings about Jeremy from *Those Shoes* are complicated. On the one hand, I think he is generous and selfless, and on the other hand, I think he cares too much about what others think." Whatever structure you choose, you will need to help each child revise his or her seed idea so that it is a clear thesis, making sure it is a claim or an idea, not a fact, phrase, or question. Implicit in all of these thesis statements is the plan for the essay, because each part of the statement can serve as the topic sentence for a different paragraph.

Guide students as they find evidence, draft, and revise a cohesive essay.

Once a child has planned his or her boxes and bullets for a literary essay, the child will need to collect the information and insights required to build the case. You can decide whether you'll encourage your writers to create physical folders for each bullet, or topic sentence, in which they can place evidence gathered on pieces of paper. For example, if the child's claim is "Cynthia Rylant's story 'Spaghetti' is the story of a lonely boy who learns from a tiny stray kitten to open himself to love," the child might title one folder, "Gabriel is a lonely boy" and another, "Gabriel learns to open himself to love." On the other hand, students can collect and write straight onto draft paper, working with one page for each bullet.

You may teach your writers to gather evidence for each of their subordinate points by retelling a part of the story that supports the idea, then "unpacking" that part, writing about how it illustrates the idea. Your writers will likely need to be taught to find evidence that supports their theses. You will want to encourage them to look for places in the text that are significant to the overall meaning of the story, because often these are the parts that best support an argument about a text. You might show students to notice when the author has spent time stretching a scene out or repeating images. You will need to help them retell those portions of the text in such a way that they angle them to fit with their ideas.

You will need to teach writers how to quote from a text and how to unpack these quotes by talking about how the quote addresses the relevant big idea. When children are doing this work, it is helpful to have extra copies of the texts or pages they are using so that children can cut out relevant parts and paste them onto their drafts and then write how that part supports the thesis. Then, writers try another part and another and another. This takes out the labor-intensive work of copying the lines and puts more emphasis on the intellectual work of considering which evidence is best suited to prove an idea, how to retell in an angled manner, and how to unpack the evidence. If you would like further references and if you have access to the fourth-grade books in this series, this work is described in great detail in *The Literary Essay: Writing about Fiction*.

Then, as you channel your writers toward drafting, remind them to transfer and apply all that they have learned about developing an essay—ordering evidence and creating introductions and conclusions that orient and engage the reader. Focus your teaching on how literary essays differ from the other kinds of essays they have written this year. For example, show them how to write introductory paragraphs that include a tiny summary of the story and then present the thesis statement. Closing paragraphs will probably be a place to link the story's message to the writer's own life. The ending is a good place for a Hallmark moment! "This story teaches me that I too . . ." An alternative is to link this story to another story, or even to a social issue in the world.

Then shift your students into revision, perhaps beginning this part of the unit by teaching them that writers read their drafts carefully—perhaps with a writing partner—looking for places where there are gaps in thinking or transitions, and then fill those gaps as they revise. One kind of gap might be a lack of evidence to support a particular point. Or the writer might have forgotten to include some language to link evidence to the point or to the thesis. Transition language will help writers to make these connections, such as "This part shows . . ." or "The actions of this character prove the point that . . ."

Finally, save some time to teach a lesson or two about editing essays. You'll want to build on the editing work you have done across the year—encouraging students to make smart choices about paragraphing and ending punctuation. This unit is a great opportunity to teach into verb tense, because oftentimes many tenses are used during an essay. When writers are discussing their thinking, they sometimes use the present tense ("Gabriel is lonely."), and when they are retelling they sometimes switch to the past tense ("Gabriel saw the cat.").

Help students self-assess and draft quick on-demand literary essays.

Before you move on to a second major essay, you may want to pause here and spend a day or two teaching students to transfer and apply all they have learned as they draft quick essays. You might launch this work using a text that you have previously read aloud, channeling your students to quickly brainstorm ideas about major and minor characters and themes as a class. Then you can put up a simple structure for planning on a chart, such as:

Idea

One part that makes me think this is . . .

This part shows . . .

Another part that makes me think this is . . .

This part shows . . .

Now I'm starting to realize . . .

You'll charge students with quickly planning an essay using one of the ideas they have brainstormed, first practicing by "writing-in-the-air" with a partner and then going off to flash-draft that essay. This work will help your students to transfer and apply what they are learning about essay writing, and it will provide practice in writing on-demand essays, which will serve them well if they encounter essays about texts on a standardized test. Next, offer writers the opportunity to assess their drafts with the Opinion Writing Checklist, using what they notice to set some goals for themselves.

BEND II: WRITE ACROSS TEXTS

Highly literate people have the ability to make comparisons across texts. This is a marker of literacy that we want for our students. Writing comparative literary essays is one way to cultivate this. Writing about more than one text offers powerful opportunities for comparing and contrasting characters and themes in stories. This work also invites students to think about how different texts can offer views on a subject that are in some ways similar and in some ways different. This kind of thinking and writing demands that a writer synthesize and analyze, and requires a writer to pay attention not only to the subject of a text but also to an author's treatment of that subject. This leads a child to notice matters of point of view, emphasis, and interpretation and to be aware of the different craft moves that the authors of the different texts have used. All of this work is very much a part of the new Common Core State Standards. You can teach students to draw upon all of that work and transfer and apply their learning to their writing.

To introduce children to the concept of comparing and contrasting two texts, you might suggest they first compare two objects. For example, students may compare a basketball and a football or a pen and a pencil. This can be done through writing-in-the-air, where students talk out how the writing would go, or it could be done through some shared writing, with the class contributing to one compare-and-contrast text. Then again, if the whole class compared and contrasted pencils and pens, each writer could think of his or her own objects and do similar work—a dog and a cat, an iPod and a radio, a Ford and a Honda. You could use the concrete presence of the items to show writers different ways to go about doing this work.

One way to proceed would be to take one item—the pen, the Honda—and to talk or write about it, touching on a few key features. Then the writer could pick up the second object—the pencil, the Ford—and try to talk about each of the same features, showing how that feature is a bit different for the second item. The interesting thing to point out for writers is that when talking about a basketball, for example, there might be all kinds of ways to describe it, but when comparing it to a football, certain qualities become more essential to the description: its shape, its color, what it is filled with, and so forth. So you could teach students that actually one can't begin with the one object and proceed to the next; instead, one needs to do some bird's-eye thinking about the two subjects, laying out the features that merit attention. This will allow students to become familiar with the structure and feel of comparison essays before asking them to work with the added complication of the two texts.

When your students move from writing about pens and pencils to writing about texts, you will need to gauge the number of days you have left in the unit to calculate the work you'll ask them to do. The quickest way to give them an immersion course in comparative essay writing might be to suggest they read a story that is in some ways like and in some ways different than the story they wrote about in their literary essay. They will have already thought deeply about one text and will probably therefore be able to fairly quickly juxtapose the second text to the first. That is, if one student has written her first essay about story A, you may channel her to write her comparative essay comparing and contrasting story A and story B. Meanwhile, if another student wrote about story B in his first essay, you may channel him to also compare and contrast story A and story B. You can find suggested stories that can be partnered in these ways in the additional resources of this document. Of course, you may create your own text sets or encourage students to decide for themselves which stories make sense for comparison. Either way, you could show students that a compare-and-contrast essay can literally be written in a single day, and of course you'd suggest writers follow the structure you taught them as they were writing about pens and pencils or Hondas and Fords.

Support students as they collect big ideas and important details.

One of the goals for this bend of the unit is to have children dig deeper into texts and write about more sophisticated interpretations. You'll want to support students in remembering that it is in the subtle nuances and details of texts that themes are developed and help them to revisit texts and annotate them with more complex interpretations.

Part of your teaching in this portion of the unit will be helping your writers to move beyond ideas that are single descriptors of characters, such as "Gabriel is a lonely boy." To continue to push students toward more complex thesis statements, teach them to revisit themes or big ideas found in earlier books and remember the work they did to come up with them. Remind your writers of work they did in the previous bend that was especially powerful, such as looking for an image or object and thinking about why and how it was used to bring out the significance of the part. Or you may want to teach them to look at moments where a character has strong feelings or reactions and think about why the character is feeling or reacting this way, and then to consider possible lessons. You can also teach your writers to pay close attention to times when characters have insights or learn something, and to search for universal lessons in these moments of insight. Any of these methods can lead to a rich, more sophisticated thesis statement.

You may decide that you can give a bit more time to this work, in which case you may specifically teach students that, just as literary essayists know ahead of time that some places are rich ground for literary analysis, they know that some things are rich ground for literary comparison. For example, writers are apt to explore the ways the theme is and is not the same across the two texts or think about ways in which characters' lessons or changes are and are not the same across the two texts. You can remind students of the work they are currently doing in reading workshop, thinking of other texts, poems, and stories that connect to the theme, and use these texts as well as ideas they have already come up with to connect to the other text.

As students work on these essays, you'll want to be ready to give some tips. One of the important things to teach is that a compare-and-contrast essay is always expected to do both—to compare and also contrast. Even if the texts are largely different, it is wise for a writer to push himself or herself to think of similarities, although these can be more minor. You may teach students to write, "These stories are similar in X and in Z," planning then to elaborate both in paragraphs that begin with topic sentences such as "Although X and Y are [some way they are different], they are similar because [they explore the same theme]."

Then again, a child could write a thesis that goes like this: "Both [title] and [title] are stories about . . . " This kind of thesis statement will lead students to write about theme, as in "Both *Those Shoes* and 'Stray' are stories about longing and learning to appreciate what you have." Or "The characters in . . . and . . . in . . . are both . . . " For example, this claim might go like this: "Both Opal from *Because of Winn-Dixie* and Doris from 'Stray' are lonely." This structure has students writing about how two characters are similar. Of course, this same structure works for differences, as in "The difference between [one character] and [another character] is . . . " or "Unlike [one character] in [title], [another character in another book] is . . . "

To take this a step further, students could also write about how both characters are similar *and* how they are different: "While both Opal from *Because of Winn-Dixie* and Doris from 'Stray' are lonely, the two characters are lonely for different reasons." Or "What's the same about these two stories or characters is . . . What's different about these two stories is . . . " Or "The characters in [title] and [title] are similar and different in several ways." Or, "Both the characters in [title] and [title] are . . . but while [one character] is . . . [the other character] is . . . " Or "Both stories, [story A] and [story B], deal with the theme of . . . but while . . . " Whatever the structure you choose, you will need to help each child revise his or her seed idea so that it is a clear thesis, making sure it is a claim or an idea, not a fact, phrase, or question, and that it works across both texts.

Support students as they develop a thesis statement and plan a draft.

As in the first literary essay, planning a comparative essay does not necessarily go just one way. Depending on the essayist's thesis statement, the plan for the essay will vary. If a student is comparing themes in the books, then the boxes and bullets may contain three reasons why these books are about this theme or three different things these books say about this theme or two reasons why the theme is similar and one reason why it is different. Or if students are writing about two characters, either in the same book or across texts, then their boxes and bullets will need to reflect that structure. Theirs might look like three ways the characters are the same or perhaps one or two ways they are the same and one way they differ.

There are two common structures for comparative essays that you may want to teach your students, and they can then decide which will work better for them. One structure is called the "block" essay structure. Using the block structure, students write one body paragraph, or one section of the body that may include more than one paragraph, all about *one* text, and use the second body paragraph or section to write about the second text. Thus, the bullets in a boxes-and-bullets plan would have one bullet for one text and one bullet for the second text. A second possible structure has more synthesized body paragraphs: each body paragraph includes discussions of *both* texts. It could be that one body paragraph explores the similarities in the texts, and another explores the differences. This structure is commonly called "point by point." An example of such a plan might be as follows.

"The Great Gilly Hopkins" and "Homecoming" show that sometimes in life, people will do anything for the ones they love.

- Mrs. Trotter will do anything for Gilly and Dicey will do anything for her brothers and sisters.
- Mrs. Trotter accepts Gilly's nastiness and turns the other cheek while Dicey won't accept the conditions her brothers and sister are forced to live in and she takes a bold stand and has them all run away.

Because it can be a very tricky thing to choose the structure of an essay, it sometimes takes a few tries before a writer finds the right fit. You may want to have a few examples, or templates, of how literary essays might be structured. You might teach your writers how to organize their supports (bullets) both in blocks and point by point.

We have included a sample essay in each format, so that both you and your students can see how they go. Your students will find it easier to plan if they can envision what the essay will look like, so taking time to study mentor texts would be worthwhile. You may use the essays as they are here or write your own using texts that are familiar to your students. Once again, the more that you and your colleagues have written your own essays together and with your students, the easier this work goes.

Support students as they find evidence.

Once a child has planned the boxes and bullets for a comparative essay, the child will need to collect the evidence and insights required to support the claim. Again, the writer will gather evidence by retelling a part of the story that supports his idea, writing a brief summary of a relevant part of the story, using lists of moments that support the idea, or explaining the craft moves that he used that reveal the idea he is asserting. For example, you might teach students that the way they retell a moment can angle it to fit their idea. Word choice becomes central to angling their stories, as does only including the parts that fit their idea. Writers can also draw on what they have learned about analyzing point of view to discuss how themes are developed differently through the way that events are described.

Alternatively, and due to the pace of this unit, you might choose to have children bypass the process of gathering information into files, instead using rough forms of outlines to plan the content of a paragraph, then writing one support paragraph on one page and the other on another page. Either way, you will probably want to have students collect quotes from the texts that support their ideas during this stage, as well.

Push students to draft, revise, and edit with independence.

As your students prepare to draft their essays, bring their minds back to all they learned while writing their first literary essays. This should feel not like brand new work for the students, but like an iteration of what they have already done. You will want to charge them with taking themselves through the process with greater independence, together creating checklists, to-do lists, and other tools, if needed, to monitor their own progress.

After they have drafted, you may want to teach students transitional phrases that support comparative essays. You will surely need to plan for small-group teaching, because students will be writing within different structures. Teaching a lesson on introductions and conclusions will likely be necessary as well. You may want to teach students how to include information about both texts in the introduction. This might look like a brief summary of both texts: "*Those Shoes* is about . . . and 'Stray' is about . . . " Or you may want to teach how essayists sometimes discuss the importance of stories in their introductions: "Both of these stories are important because . . . " For their conclusions, some may sum up what was said already and then close with inspirational lines. These lines may be similar to what they learned earlier: they might comment on a social issue connected to the theme from the books explored in the essay, or they might connect the ideas in the essay to the writer's life. Others may explore the differences between the two texts, especially if the bodies of their essays explored only the similarities. For example, you might teach how the stories end in different ways or that while characters are similar in their traits or desires, their reasons for their feelings may differ.

Just as students did when revising their first literary essays, they will want to read their drafts carefully—most likely with a writing partner—looking for places where there are gaps in thinking or transitions, and fill those gaps as they revise. As students are doing large-scale revisions on their drafts, you might now rally them to revisit the drafts of their literary essays and revise these using all they have learned across this unit. You might remind writers to reconsider their goals using the Opinion Writing Checklist. By self-assessing their work against expectations, students can revise all of their drafts to ensure that each piece of writing reveals all of their newest learning and therefore is an example of their best work.

BEND III: EDIT AND PUBLISH: PREPARE ESSAYS TO SHARE WITH THE WORLD

You will surely want to help students polish their essays with one or two lessons on editing. Comparative essays provide an opportunity for exploring complex sentence structures. Teaching a lesson on appositive commas or beginning sentences with dependent clauses will help students' writing to sound more sophisticated.

For a celebration of the writing, you might have students lay their first literary essay and their comparative essay side by side, and have students visit each other's writing, complimenting as they go. Or you might set up a rotating display in the classroom that highlights the two books as a pair, with the comparative essays tucked inside one of the books, creating a suggested path for reading for others in the class. You could also consider posting their essays on Goodreads.com.

ADDITIONAL RESOURCES
Sample Essay 1

Block structure:

- Introduction
- Story 1 and its analysis
- Story 2 and its analysis
- Conclusion

In "Those Shoes," by Maribeth Boelts, and "Stray," by Cynthia Rylant, we meet two characters whose longing for something that their families cannot afford brings them close to despair, but then sheds a different light on what is already in their worlds but not fully appreciated or explored. Reading these two stories has made me realize that although we may search outside of ourselves and our relationships for happiness, there is nothing so valuable as our connections to the people closest to us, and nothing so fulfilling as strengthening those connections.

In the story "Those Shoes," Jeremy longs for a pair of shoes that his grandmother tells him they just can't afford. But Jeremy sees "those shoes" everywhere—it seems that all the other boys are wearing them, and Jeremy can't escape the message that without the black high-tops with two white stripes, he just isn't fast enough, cool enough, or popular enough to count. "I have dreams about those shoes," he says. He wants the shoes so much that he pays for a second-hand pair of them himself, even though they pinch his toes because they are the wrong size. It is clear that Jeremy hopes that "those shoes" will make up for all the other differences between himself and the other boys, differences that he can't control and that he knows his grandmother can't control either. Along the way, however, Jeremy discovers that even without the shoes, he is loved and he can be happy. By the end of the story, when he has finally given the shoes away to a boy who was kind to him, he realizes that the boots his grandmother bought for him are just right for the moment. We can see that he's starting to appreciate what his grandmother does give him, rather than worrying about what she can't give him.

Doris in "Stray" finds a puppy in the aftermath of a huge snowstorm and wants to keep it so badly, even though she knows that "her father made so little money any pets were out of the question." Doris pushes herself to tell her parents about it, even though she understands that her father is determined to take the dog to the pound as soon as the snow has been cleared and he can get his truck out; even when her parents ignore her, she keeps saying more about the dog and how easy it would be to keep it. Doris's dreams, like Jeremy's, are affected by her impossible wish: "Her dreams were full of searching and searching for things lost." As readers, we are suspicious of her parents, as they seem unnecessarily harsh and uncaring. Like Doris, we feel that her parents don't see her needs and we resent them for it. In a surprise ending, however, Doris's father returns from the pound and has brought the puppy back with him. He was unable, he says, to leave it in such a horrible place. Doris is speechless, and she understands, as we do too, that her parents do see her needs, and that they are capable of love even if it is costly. Although the return of the dog is miraculous, this new appreciation for her parents is the true joy for Doris.

These stories end in very different ways. In each case, however, the reader can understand that the human relationships in these characters' lives are what matter most, and that it is the strength of those relationships that we trust to bring future happiness to Jeremy and Doris, despite the harsh material conditions of their lives. We can trust that, although, as Jeremy's grandmother says, "There's no room for 'want' around here—just need," Jeremy and Doris will get what they need, which is the love of the people around them.

Sample Essay 2

Point-by-point structure:

- Introduction
- Subordinate claim #1 as it applies to both texts
- Subordinate claim #2 as it applies to both texts
- Conclusion

Jeremy, in the story "Those Shoes," by Maribeth Boelts, wants a pair of sneakers that are too expensive for his grandmother to buy new. By the end of the story, Jeremy learns that he doesn't need the shoes to be happy, that there are other parts of his life that matter. In Cynthia Rylant's moving story "Stray," Doris is a young girl who finds a puppy during a snowstorm and sets her heart on keeping him, although she knows her parents won't hear of it. This story's happy ending rests more on Doris's realization that her parents really care about her than on the fact that she gets to keep the dog. "Those Shoes," by Maribeth Boelts and "Stray" by Cynthia Rylant are both stories of longing and acceptance: Both are stories of characters who want something extraordinary, but end up appreciating what they already have.

In both stories, we are introduced to characters who desperately desire something that their families cannot afford. Jeremy sees "those shoes" everywhere—it seems that all the other boys are wearing them, and Jeremy can't escape the message that without the black high-tops with two white stripes, he just isn't fast enough, cool enough, or popular enough to count. "I have dreams about those shoes," he says. He wants the shoes so much that he pays for a second-hand pair of them himself, even though they pinch his toes because they are the wrong size. Doris wants to keep the puppy she finds so badly, even though she knows that "her father made so little money any pets were out of the question." Doris pushes herself to tell her parents about it, even though she understands that her father is determined to take the dog to the pound as soon as the snow has been cleared and he can get his truck out; even when her parents ignore her, she keeps saying more about the dog and how easy it would be to keep it. Doris's dreams, like Jeremy's, are affected by her impossible wish: "Her dreams were full of searching and searching for things lost."

Both characters, however, come to terms with their searching by the end of the stories. The stories have very different outcomes for the characters: Jeremy's wish is never fulfilled, whereas Doris's is. Jeremy eventually decides to give his too-small shoes away to a boy who has been kind to him when others were making fun. Doris spends a terrible afternoon trying to adjust to the loss of the puppy, only to discover that evening that her father has brought the dog back home after all. In each case, the reader can understand that the human relationships in these characters' lives are what matter most, and that it is the strength of those relationships that we trust to bring future happiness to Jeremy and Doris, despite the harsh material conditions of their lives. By the end of *Those Shoes*, it has snowed, and Jeremy remembers that his grandmother has bought new boots for him. "New black boots that no kid has ever worn before." And by the end of "Stray," the snow has cleared and Doris's parents have changed their minds—we see a new side of Doris's dad, who couldn't bear to leave the dog in the cruel pound.

Reading these two stories has made me realize that although we may search outside of ourselves and our relationships for happiness, there is nothing so valuable as our connections to the people closest to us, and nothing so fulfilling as strengthening those connections. We can trust that, although, as Jeremy's grandmother says, "There's no room for 'want' around here—just need," Jeremy and Doris will get what they need, which is the love of the people around them.

Poetry Anthologies
Writing, Thinking, and Seeing More

INTRODUCTION/RATIONALE

A poetry unit is an exciting time in the writing workshop. No other genre grants young writers quite the same freedom to experiment with space on the page, to savor the sound of the words they are writing, and above all, to make universal meaning out of close observations, thoughts, and questions about the world and personal experience. A poetry unit of study ushers your students into a new world of making meaning: a world that fosters deep connections between reading and writing and a commitment to repeated revision. This year, your poetry unit could also emphasize collecting poems around a particular theme or topic as a way to push students to write more, think more deeply, and explore various points of view. Writing interrelated poems is more complex work than writing poems that do not connect to one another. In this way, too, this work is more sophisticated than the poetry work of previous years.

This unit offers a unique opportunity to zoom in on craft from both the reader's and the writer's perspective. Although poets, like all authors, write to find and communicate meaning, they engage the reader in the surface of the language, the way words look on the page and sound to the ear, more than many writers of prose do. As your kids try out a number of poems on a chosen topic or theme, they will have a chance to experience firsthand how differently crafted texts can offer truly different perspectives on the same subject.

In this unit, you'll invite children to write poems in response to the topics and themes that surround them: poems about finding and losing friends, the power of sports to heal and to devastate. You'll teach children to find the poems that are hiding in the details of their lives. You'll do all this not just because poetry is its own powerful genre but also because the habits children develop as poets—specificity, comparative thinking, understatement, and hyperbole—will serve them well when writing any genre.

Watch for your English language learners to flourish in this unit. Poetry is relatively flexible in terms of grammar, and more can be communicated with fewer words than within the conventions of prose. This often makes poetry more accessible to writers learning

English. Then too, their familiarity with one or more other languages gives them a wider array of grammatical structures, cadences, words, and sounds to draw from as they create their poetry. Expect that *all* your children will bring their own voice to the poems they will create in your room this month—and be ready to celebrate these voices when you see them emerge. Expect too that, whatever the format of publication, every child will draft, revise, and edit several poems, using mentor texts and your lessons as guides throughout the process.

An understanding of poetry from the inside out will help students build a lasting mental framework for how poetry works and support their ability to read poetry with comprehension and craft appreciation, skills that are expected by the Common Core State Standards and the National Assessment of Educational Progress.

You'll want to take this unit as an opportunity to teach the work called for by the Common Core State Standards in reading. For instance, in looking closely at anthologies that include poems from different points of view, your students will also be practicing compare and contrast at a fifth grade level. Then too, the Common Core State Standards expect that our young readers will develop their understanding and appreciation of not only what the author of a text is saying but also how that text gets that meaning across. A unit on poetry also helps students internalize the structural elements of poems (e.g., verse, rhythm, meter), thus preparing them to explain and analyze the major differences between poems, drama, and prose.

A SUMMARY OF THE BENDS IN THE ROAD FOR THIS UNIT

In Bend I (Create a Class Anthology), you will spend several days creating a class anthology around a common theme, demonstrating ways to take on different perspectives and approaches within the same topic. This will set the tone for the students' own work, teaching them that anthologies can be created with a mission to explore a topic from a number of points of view, through different kinds of poetry.

In Bend II (Generate Ideas for Anthologies and Collect Poems), you will spend a few more days helping kids gather ideas for their own anthologies and try out some poems to go with those topics. You will teach children ways to select poems for an anthology and ways to revise toward the bigger theme, perhaps writing new poems to round out their ideas or frameworks. During this generating stage, you will most likely introduce a few strategies for first-try poetry. Then, in a mid-workshop teaching point or share, you'll quickly show how poets don't wait for revision, that any first try is open for rethinking and reworking. Using published poems as mentors during this bend will help you maintain a sense of exploration and inspiration as your young poets strive to mimic the work of published authors.

In Bend III (Get Strong Drafts Going and Revise All Along), you will continue to emphasize the fact that drafting and revising go hand in hand. Children will continue to write new poems but also spend time revisiting and revising. You'll encourage children to zoom in on a small collection of poems on which to apply revision strategies (these will later become their anthologies). You will teach them to turn prose into poetry by focusing on structure and to revise to bring out the intended meaning of each poem.

In Bend IV (Edit Poems and Assemble Anthologies for Publication), you will spend some days coaching children on ways to prepare for publication. In addition to editing, this may mean creating illustrations to go with the central images of the poems they've written or rehearsing reading their poems aloud in a way that makes their meaning clear to the audience. Children will also refine their work in ways that are appropriate to the form of publication you've chosen.

GETTING READY
Gather Texts

To start off the unit, you'll want to create an environment in which children read, hear, and speak poetry. Perhaps you'll bring in baskets of fresh, new poems, poetry books, and poetry anthologies for your classroom library. You will need to have many examples of different kinds of poems on hand! You might recruit the school librarian to help students find, read, and reread poems they love. Don't forget your public library. Try to find anthologies that are focused on a common topic or theme, such as *This Place I Know: Poems of Comfort*, edited by Georgia Heard; *Extra Innings: Baseball Poems*, by Lee Bennett Hopkins; or *If You're Not Here, Please Raise Your Hand: Poems about School*, by Kalli Dakos. Or you might find anthologies that are focused on a science subject, such as *Fine Feathered Friends*, by Jane Yolen (Yolen has written many anthologies that focus on a specific element in nature), or on a social studies subject, such as *Roots and Blues: A Celebration*, by Arnold Adoff. If you do not have many of these books, you will need to create a few folders of connected poems (you might enlist kids to help you with this). If you teach in a Spanish-English bilingual classroom or if you have many Spanish-speaking students, you may want to include some Spanish-English anthologies, and there are many lovely examples: *Gathering the Sun*, by Alma Flor Ada, and *Laughing Tomatoes and Other Spring Poems/Jitomates Risuenos y Otros Poemas de Primavera*, by Francisco X. Alarcón, are just two. You may want to explore the Poetry Foundation, an independent literary organization, whose website (www.poetryfoundation.org) includes a children's poetry section and honors a new children's poet laureate every two years.

Immersion will play a larger role in this unit than in other writing units, from the very start of the unit and all the way through. Because you will want to teach your kids to read poems well and thoughtfully, in addition to teaching them how to use those poems as mentors, you will want to pick some touchstones that serve both purposes well.

You'll also want to make use of the many wonderful professional texts available. These texts will help you imagine the possibilities for the work students will do and the ways you can best support their growth in this important genre. Here are a few professional texts we recommend:

Awakening the Heart: Exploring Poetry in Elementary and Middle School, by Georgia Heard

A Note Slipped Under the Door: Teaching from Poems We Love, by Nick Flynn and Shirley McPhillips

Handbook of Poetic Forms, edited by Ron Padgett

Wham! It's a Poetry Jam: Discovering Performance Poetry, by Sara Holbrook

A Kick in the Head: An Everyday Guide to Poetic Forms, edited by Paul B. Janeczko

Getting the Knack: 20 Poetry Writing Exercises, by Stephen Dunning and William Stafford

Choose When and How Children Will Publish

Where, for whom, and in what format will children publish their poetry? How will they celebrate? This will, in part, be based on what you discover after conducting an on-demand assessment; your decision will also be based on what's realistic for the time you have carved out and your access to materials and publishing/performance space. As the unit approaches its end, you may invite your poets to make choices about how they will share their poems with others. In some classrooms, students choose to decorate and post their poems in public places around the school and neighborhood. Other classes invite parents and schoolmates to join in a poetry slam, where children read and perform their poems aloud. Other classes may choose to simply compile their poems into an anthology and place it in the classroom or school library.

BEND I: CREATE A CLASS ANTHOLOGY

You'll begin this unit by creating a class anthology of poems around a topic of common interest, all in a few days of quick-drafting and revision. On the first day of the unit, you might read aloud *This Is Just to Say: Poems of Apology and Forgiveness*, by Joyce Sidman. In this fictional story, a class of sixth-graders write poems of apology and forgiveness after their teacher reads them the poem "This Is Just to Say," by William Carlos Williams, and then create their own anthology. After reading a few poems from the book, you might say, "We could try something just like this!" As a class you would then quickly brainstorm some possible topics or themes for the class anthology.

You might show how a topic can have several embedded themes: baseball, for example, might include themes like "it's hard to let your team down," "practice makes perfect," and "sometimes no matter how hard you try, you still don't win." Then enlist students to write poems that get at these different themes. You'll need to spend a little time coming to consensus around a topic, and then make sure children all have picked themes or messages they want to try out. It doesn't matter if there is overlap: more than one writer can take up the same theme! One poet might choose to write several poems about one theme. Another might choose to write one poem about how "practice makes perfect" and another poem about how "sometimes no matter how hard you try, you still don't win." The logistics are not as important as making sure that students write, write, write. Ultimately, the point of this work is to give students practice using poetry to get across meaning.

You'll want to plan three or four minilessons to teach in this bend. To model the strategies, you might choose one of the themes and write in front of children, letting them inside the process of your writing. You might model zooming in on small moments and vivid images that are tied to the meaning you hope to convey. You might teach children a few of the ways poets use line breaks—to show shifts in time or setting, for dramatic effect, or to influence the way a reader reads the poem. Then, too, you might teach your young poets that they can use all they know about narrative writing when they write poetry. That is to say, poets use dialogue, internal thinking, descriptive details, and other craft moves to bring out what a poem is really about. You'll want to emphasize that the qualities of good writing span genres.

Surround your writers with mentor texts, not just by lining the bookshelves with popular poetry anthologies but by displaying poems around the room—perhaps even having a Poem of the Day display that keeps changing. Mid-workshop teaching points would be well spent delving into some of these texts and sharing how two very different poems about the same topic—"Dreams," by Langston Hughes, and "Listen to the Mustn'ts," by Shel Silverstein, for example—get at different sides of the topic. Hughes's poem is dark and suggests that without our imagination, we are lost; Silverstein is more hopeful, letting the reader know that dreaming is always possible, even when others are naysayers. You can teach students to consider who the speaker might be in each of these poems and what we can tell about the speaker from the ideas that come through in the poem. It's also a good time to teach students that the poet and the speaker may or may not be the same person: that poets can take on the voice or "persona" of someone else. Invite them to try this in their own poems as well.

BEND II: GENERATE IDEAS FOR ANTHOLOGIES AND COLLECT POEMS

During the next week or so, you will want to teach students ways to come up with topics for their individual anthologies and help them write poems exploring different perspectives on those topics.

The generating process is as diverse as poetry itself. Poems can grow out of observations or emotions, out of memories and images, or from a clever turn of phrase that is borrowed, overheard, or invented out of the blue. Poems may grow out of or respond to other poems. They may grow out of a story or stem from the writer's concern about an issue or need to make a difference. As with personal narrative, you won't want to inundate your children with these strategies. Instead, introduce three or four as you teach writers how to use their notebooks as a place to begin collecting ideas and poems. You'll want the choice of theme to feel deliberate and intentional and be one about which the children have some strong feelings or investment.

Continue to look at poems together and give your kids time to wander in the poetry books and anthologies that are in your room. Often, reading poetry with a partner (first aloud, then silently) and discussing it can spark conversations that will lead to fast and furious writing of original poems. You may model how a mentor poem can lead to a poem about the same topic, a poem that follows the same structure, or a poem that talks back to the original poem.

You will want to select a variety of poems to share with the whole class, so that you do not reinforce your kids' ideas that poetry has to look or sound a certain way. Choose a selection of poems from a couple of anthologies that showcase different effects a group of poems can have. For example, a Jack Prelutsky book may include poems loosely connected by the humor, whereas Lee Bennett Hopkins's baseball collection has a more explicit topical connection with more diversity of emotion and style. In addition to these touchstones, of course, you will need a much broader selection of poetry books and folders of poetry that students can read independently and use as models.

Combing through previous notebook entries may evoke inspiration. "Flipping through the pages of your previous writing might lead you to poems that are hiding in the words, waiting to be written," you might say, urging your young poets to pry previous notebook entries apart with a pencil, to circle or copy out a line or a paragraph they might turn into a poem. You will remind them that writers return to the same themes again and again and that perusing old entries through this lens should engender some "aha" moments and ideas for new work: "I'm always writing about being disappointed in my brother. Maybe I could write an anthology with poems that get at all the ways I'm feeling about him, to see if I can come up with more than those disappointed feelings."

Looking at images or going on observation walks (in a park or nature preserve, in the community, in the building) with notebook and pen in hand is another way for children to observe and imagine what they might write about. Teach them to first write long about what they see, what they notice, and what this makes them think. Above all, you will try to teach—and model—a thoughtfulness and a wakefulness that is essential to getting a poem going. Nothing you say need be very poetic or profound as long as you uninhibitedly model a sense of being alert to the visual details around you.

Many teachers have successfully started a poetry unit by bringing in song lyrics and inviting children to bring in the (appropriate) lyrics to music they are obsessed with. This is a way both to notice how songs actually are poems (including line breaks, repetition, figurative language, and rhyme schemes) and to inspire new writing based on the lyrics' theme or image. You might share a pair of mismatched love songs ("Love Hurts" and "Love Is All You Need") as a way to show how different songwriters angle their work to give different meanings. Just as some poems originate in ideas and images, some begin, quite literally, with words. A catchy phrase or a lyrical line can play in a poet's head and eventually spur a bigger idea.

You will expect your writers, after a day or two of generating or collecting, to end up with lots of small blurbs and/or first tries, all waiting to become better-crafted poems. Often, these kinds of gathering entries may not start out looking like poems, instead taking the shape of small paragraphs, perhaps like story blurbs for narratives or small patches of thought for essays. This is fine—and to be expected. These entries are initial fodder for powerful poems; they will not arrive in final and perfected form. It's also fine if children are using line breaks and creating entries that *do* look poetic right away. What is important is that children learn to generate ideas that have power and resonance for them.

During the generating stage, you will most likely introduce a few strategies for first-try poetry, then in a mid-workshop teaching point or share, quickly show how poets don't wait for revision, that any first try is open for rethinking and reworking. You may then choose to teach a generating lesson that shows how a first try can spawn new thinking that leads to the writing of a whole new poem, not just changing a word here and there—a new poem that perhaps offers a slightly different perspective on the same topic. In this way you will continue to support an important trend in your writing workshop: writing with volume, which in poetry probably means writing lots of poems and lots of versions of poems rather than writing long poems.

In a mid-workshop teaching point or a share during these first couple of days you could introduce the idea of on-the-run revision in poetry. You might teach students that poets don't wait until it's "time to revise" to rethink and recraft. You might use an in-process poem of your own. For example, right away I can look at these lines I just wrote about a fight I had with my brother:

> He was so mad
> he threw a shoe
> into the basement wall.
> I was scared of his anger
> as usual.

and add an image from the setting or a detail about an object or piece of clothing that will make the poem more piercing. Poets especially look for a surprising detail or one that adds a new emotion to the poem. You might remind children how in personal narrative, in fiction, in information writing—in every kind of writing—they worked on bringing in important details. Poetry is no different. In this case, I might demonstrate, closing my eyes, picturing the hole in the wall in our basement, and adding some lines.

> He was so mad
> he threw a shoe
> into the basement wall.
> The shoe thumped to the ground,
> leaving a hole, ragged and dark
> between my brother and me.
> I was scared of his anger
> as usual.

Let your students know that as the unit progresses, they will need to go back and collect more entries so that they can write more poems. They need to do this because as their ideas for their anthologies start to shift, they'll need new poems to fill out their ideas. For example, if I'm writing about the troubles of having a brother, I might now need a poem from his perspective or maybe from my mom's perspective (or even the wall's perspective!), and I'll have to write those.

62

BEND III: GET STRONG DRAFTS GOING AND REVISE ALL ALONG

Early on, you might also encourage children to talk with their partners and write reflectively about the entries they have collected in their notebooks. Children may reflect by writing or saying, "I'm writing about this because . . . " or "I want my reader to feel or think . . . " or "One thing that may be missing here is . . . " This work helps children uncover the deeper meaning in their entries and begin to plan for a collection of poems that shows different sides of their chosen topics or themes.

Now that students have several short entries chock full of meaningful moments, observations, and ideas, you can invite them to draft these more formally and experiment with the craft of poets. You will probably emphasize free verse at the beginning. Rhyming well is a precise skill that many adult poets find difficult to master! Teach children to aim first for meaning and for finding a way to describe what matters with words that will make the reader see the world in a brand-new way. You will want to teach students how to draft the bare bones, the preliminary sketch, of a poem out of the ideas they've generated.

Help students turn prose into poetry by focusing on structure.

Model for students how to mold poems from previous notebook entries or other writing generated in prose. "Poets know how to turn prose into poetry," you might say, showing them that they can discover rhythm in the sentences they've jotted by breaking them up. For example, you might put one of the blurbs you've written up on chart paper or a document camera and read it aloud.

> I was running in the park with my friends, and we were all running together at first. But because I had allergies, I had trouble keeping up with them. Soon I was all by myself, watching my friends run farther away from me. I felt so weak and alone.

"This is not a poem," you'll tell kids, "but I can make it a poem by breaking it into lines. When I take a sentence and stop part way through and write the rest on the next line, I am making what poets call a *line break*." You might continue, "Let's look at my entry about running and make it into a poem by adding line breaks. Wherever I want to put a line break, I am going to insert a little slash. I'm going to add a few and then ask you and your partner to help me." You might turn back to the chart and begin adding, all the while thinking out loud: "'I was running in the park.' That sounds like a good line. I'll break there."

> I was running in the park/with my friends,/and we were all running together at first./But because I had allergies,/I had trouble keeping up with them.

You would then ask students to help you add other line breaks into your poem, reminding them how mentor poems you've read helped you make choices about line breaks. You might explain, "I know from the poems I've read that sometimes lines breaks go where there are end marks, sometimes they go after important words, and sometimes poets use line breaks just where they think it sounds good to pause." Next, show your class how you can quickly rewrite a draft of your poem, going to a new line at each slash mark:

> I was running in the park
> with my friends
> and we were all running together at first.
> But because I had allergies,
> I had trouble keeping up with them.

Beginning with structural changes to their prose pieces will help students very quickly see their potential as poets. Experimenting with making lines and stanzas will quickly create the visual look of a poem. From there, you will decide which kinds of work to demonstrate for the whole class and which make for good small-group work or individual conferences.

You might also choose to demonstrate for the whole class how cutting lines, or cutting and pasting lines in a different order, can change the tone of a poem. Poets eliminate extra words or repeated ideas and get right to the important stuff. Instead of:

> I was running in the park/with my friends/and we were all running together at first.

Try:

> We were all running together/at first.

Or, in your model poem, you might show how more syllables in a line can give a breathless, fast-paced feeling, so you might choose that for a line that has a lot of action or where there is a rushed feeling.

> In the park we were all running together at first

But you might add more frequent line breaks—and end up with shorter lines with fewer syllables—in a part of the poem that is quieter or where you want the reader to go more slowly.

> My breathing got harder and
> I started to fall
> behind.
> Soon
> I was
> alone.

As you teach kids how playing with the length of a line affects how poets read their work, you might touch on the idea of meter. Meter—the number of beats/syllables in a given line, plus the pattern of those syllables—will likely be a new or still shaky concept for students in fourth and fifth grade, but using and understanding poetic devices is something the CCSS value.

Poets convey their ideas visually, and children can decide how long or short to make their lines on the page, whether there are stanzas or not and how many, which words are capitalized, and what kinds of punctuation to use. Children will learn how poets use the white space around the words to pause, take a breath, and make something stand out from all the other words.

Teach students to revise for meaning and create anthologies with a range of perspectives.

Once children have a few strong drafts going, you'll want to teach them poetic techniques for revision, craft moves that will amplify the messages in their poems (and support Common Core requirements for understanding poetic terminology). Their goal will be to create a collection of poems with different tones and perspectives. Drafting a poem or two of your own in front of the class will allow you to demonstrate revision strategies. Aim for children to see clearly what you did, to understand how they might do the same, and also to appreciate how this move made your poem better.

You might begin by channeling your writers to recall revision strategies they *already know* from their earlier narrative and even essay units. For example, they could try starting right in the moment instead of summarizing everything about their subject. They could try being more precise about their choice of words. You'll want to teach your students that poets, like story writers, convey meaning through imagery (you might recall writing using comparisons, tucking in the term *simile*), but that they also convey meaning through the sounds of words. Poets can express their thoughts and feelings through the way they make a line *sound*. They might choose harsh, plosive sounds or smooth, sibilant sounds. Their lines might have rhymes between them or even within them. You might show students published poets who are really skilled at rhyming, like Jack Prelutsky, and teach them that to rhyme is a choice, not a requirement, of poetry. Children might be surprised when you point out that choosing *which* words in a poem will rhyme is an important decision. Your poets might also revise for sound by thinking carefully about the choices they have made about repetition.

Another powerful revision strategy students might recall from what they know about reading poems is to consider how the ending of a poem impacts its meaning. Remind your poets that the last moments of a poem are a gift to the reader and usually leave a special image in the reader's mind or reveal the poet's main idea or perspective. A poet may reread her poem and decide on either a fitting last line or a last line that turns the tables on the rest of the poem. Just as in narrative and essay writing, young poets will want to try out various ways their poems could end.

The list of revision strategies you might potentially direct your poets toward is long, and children will no doubt take to writing poetry in varying ways. To help boost their independence, you'll want to remind your poets to apply their revision strategies to all the poems in their anthologies. Tone and word choice, for example, are work for not just one but all their poems. And since they are trying to create a range of perspectives and tones for their collections, it will be important to use the same or similar strategies toward different goals. If in one poem a child is trying to find as many harsh words as possible to get across how abrasive his brother's anger can be ("he cracked his G.I. Joe against the Jeep"), in a different poem, when remembering that same brother as the little kid he used to protect, he might search for soft-sounding words instead ("the breeze swept soft ringlets of hair into his eyes").

Partner work will be important to keep energy up during revision; you might have partners help each other by giving feedback and even recommending next steps. Your young poets won't be able to contain the urge to read their poems aloud, and partners can either listen or, better yet, read the poem back to the poet to see whether the words sound the way the poet hoped they would. Partners can also notice where there may be holes in a poet's plan for an anthology. In an anthology about school, a partner might note that all the poems seem to be from girls' perspectives. Couldn't the poet try a poem in the voice of a boy? In other words, partners can coach each other to try out the teaching you've already done.

As students meet with their partners to read and revise their poetry collections, you will want to urge them to play with punctuation. They might refer to inquiry charts on punctuation. You also want students to challenge one another on the true meaning of their poems. If they want the mood of the poem to be sad, they might decide that it is best to have fewer exclamation points. For example, you might say, "Exclamation points make everything sound upbeat and exciting; they won't fit here," and suggest they add more periods and perhaps a dash to show long pauses. Students might plan to use commas to break apart a list of things or to add more detail-supplying words to their lines: "The bright, yellow leaf died as it drifted, softly, quietly to the ground."

Finally, revision is a perfect time, if you choose, to look at a few standard forms of poetry. Once students have lived with their notebook entries for some time, you might invite them to experiment with how a haiku or pantoum, say, might enhance what they are trying to say and make it feel really powerful and purposeful. Choosing to work on form near the end of the unit, not the beginning, means that students are making *choices* about how and when to use different forms rather than simply filling in blanks to get the right number of syllables.

BEND IV: EDIT POEMS AND ASSEMBLE ANTHOLOGIES FOR PUBLICATION

Teaching students to look for rules of standard English when editing poetry can be tricky, because children's mentor poems might break these rules. It's important, therefore, to help your poets understand that while poetry can break rules, poetry also makes its own new rules—and that's what makes it extra fun sometimes. Just as you probably stressed in relation to their narrative writing, you will want to teach your poets to edit with their readers in mind. Poets make purposeful choices about grammar, spelling, and punctuation, and then they stick to those rules. For instance, a young poet might decide to go to a new line at the end of every idea instead of using a period. When she edits, she will check that she always does this. Another writer might choose to capitalize following standard rules and will check for this.

Children will probably read their poems aloud several times to make sure they sound just right. Again, they should focus on helping their readers understand what they wanted to say by checking that they have used all the punctuation marks, lines breaks, and kinds of words they need to make their poems sound just as they intended.

As your poets assemble their anthologies, they might need support choosing which poems to publish. Channel your writers to think about subjects around which they might group their poems, or ask them to select the kinds of poems they like best. Children might also decide to include the mentor poems they used or other published poems that fit within their theme. You might even invite your students to create anthologies that are not solely poems. The world of literature is full of texts that blend poetry with other genres. For example, books like *Out of the Dust*, by Karen Hesse, and *Amber Was Brave, Essie Was Smart*, by Vera B. Williams, tell stories through poems. Still other books, like *Toad by the Road*, by Joanne Ryder; Joyce Sidman's *Dark Emperor and Other Poems of the Night*; and the Yolen and Adoff examples mentioned earlier mix poems with informational text. Your poets might cling closely to a mentor anthology and write and revise other kinds of text to accompany the poems they have included.

You will want to support your writers in deciding on an order for the poems in their anthologies as well. Children might return to mentor anthologies at this point, taking a close look at how poems are organized and pausing to consider, "What if this poem were in a different place? What would the effect be of reading it earlier or later than the surrounding poems?" Then partners can have similar conversations about their own work, coming to final decisions about placement only after having reflected and reconsidered.

As the unit approaches celebration, you may invite your poets to make choices about how they will share their anthologies with others. In some classrooms this takes the form of decorating and posting poems in public places throughout the school and neighborhood. In addition to publishing the anthologies, you may want to consider incorporating a performance aspect to your celebration; students might pick a poem they have written and/or a favorite mentor poem to memorize and perform during the celebration. Poetry is multisensory: create a celebration that reflects the many dimensions of poetry.

As you prepare for the celebration, keep in mind that when you have students illustrating or decorating their work, it's especially important that you teach these activities; simply making drawings for the sake of sprucing up an anthology ranks low in Webb's Depth of Knowledge hierarchy. You can push students to use higher levels of thinking if, for example, you teach them to consider how visuals can either support the tone of the poem or offer another lens, or how the decisions they make about which poems get placed next to one another can change the way the reader will approach them.

This might also be a good opportunity to invite students to carry some of their biggest discoveries about themselves as writers into different genres. A writer might go back to an entry from, say, September or October that fits within her theme and revise it, considering not only the meaning but also the sound of their sentences. An excerpt could find its way into her anthology.

Journalism

INTRODUCTION/RATIONALE

Teachers who have taught this unit report with glee the remarkably high engagement of their students, as well as their productivity and increased focus as writers. You could teach a unit on journalism in such a way as to achieve a variety of goals. This particular spin on the unit helps students learn to write information texts quickly, to revise purposefully and swiftly, and to write from positions of thoughtful observation within their community. The unit imagines that you teach your class first to write concise, focused reports that tell the who, what, where, and when with a sense of drama. A typical news report might feature headlines such as "Spider Gets Loose from Science Lab" or "Tears During Dodgeball."

Later in the unit, you'll support students in writing news stories with more independence, helping them get a firm grasp on this, and then you'll up the ante, setting your students up to become involved in deeper investigative journalism projects. Within this portion of the unit, you'll teach them to conduct interviews and collect observation notes, to ask questions, to ponder the meaning of everyday happenings, and to write in ways that suggest significance. Investigative pieces, in contrast to news stories, may have titles such as "Spiders Get a Bum Rap at P.S. 4" or "Dodge Ball Teaches Toughness."

A SUMMARY OF THE BENDS IN THE ROAD FOR THIS UNIT

In Bend I (Generate News Stories), children will learn the basics of journalism writing. They'll learn that journalists observe a newsworthy story, and then report on it by telling the "who," "what," "where," and "when." They'll learn the importance of choosing precise details that convey the facts of the story while also hooking the reader, and they'll have a chance to revise their writing, paying attention to word count and word choice and aiming to write lean accounts.

In Bend II (Revise News Stories for Structure and Tone), children will have a chance to write yet more news stories, this time with greater attention to crafting succinct, dramatic pieces. Students will learn about the structure of a news story and how to craft engaging leads comprised of essential information followed by in-depth descriptions of the event. During the revision process, students will fine-tune the officious tone and concise language of their stories.

In Bend III (Cycle with Purpose through a Journalist's Process), students will further hone their skills in writing news stories. They will learn how to conduct interviews to add accuracy, authentic quotes, and balanced reporting to the story. They will practice how to create leads that engage readers and endings that bring closure. In this bend, students will write one to two news stories with greater purpose and skill.

In Bend IV (Edit and Publish), students will work with partners to edit each other's news stories, checking not only for conventions and paragraphing, but also for journalistic structure and content. Small groups might work together to polish headlines and create mini-newspapers, possibly even adding illustrations or photographs, to share with the school in celebration.

GETTING READY
Write and Gather Demonstration Texts

Before beginning this unit, you will probably want to enlist the help of a colleague to create a newsworthy drama in your classroom.

You might also gather news stories that illustrate the features that you plan to highlight in your minilessons: attention-grabbing headlines, leads that convey the essential information, and so on. As you select texts, you needn't think about the *topics* of the texts but instead think about the *organizational structure* and the tone of the texts. You'll want to choose news stories that resemble those you hope your children will write.

Consider How and When Your Children Will Publish

You will want to consider your options for how children will publish their news stories. One option is to create a mini-newspaper that you can share with other classrooms or the whole school. For a celebration, you might invite another class to join yours and have students share favorite parts of their news stories. You might also consider how to involve students more in the creation of the mini-newspaper. Who will design the layout? How should the news stories be grouped? What about cartoons or other illustrations? There are a variety of ways you could do this, and the main thing to remember is that students should feel that their writing is being sent out into the world to be read by others.

BEND I: GENERATE NEWS STORIES

Stage a drama in the classroom.

One attention-grabbing way to start the unit is to create a scene—to stage a drama—perhaps between yourself and another teacher, designed to provoke a reaction in your students, to get them to sit up, take note, and think, "Now that's newsworthy!" For example, another teacher in the grade might enter your room during read-aloud and begin snooping through your desk. Continue reading but show signs that you're distracted by her nosing through your stuff. Finally, look up and say, "Do you need help?" Your colleague might respond, "I'm looking for my math book. Did you borrow it and forget to return it?" Assure her that you haven't seen it, and resume reading. The teacher can continue rummaging and perhaps help herself to your favorite pens, saying, "I'm borrowing your colors because I know you have my math book somewhere." By now, students should be shocked—perhaps even outraged on your behalf.

This is just one possibility. You can figure out your own scenario. One teacher, for instance, became frightened when she "saw" a mouse in the classroom. Another had the principal come in, seize one of the books in the classroom library, and declare that it was banned. The simulation should be short and dramatic, with some kind of physical as well as verbal interaction, so that students can observe (they don't know it isn't real!). The teachers who played out these scenarios used their bodies to show their fear or their hands to show disbelief, and they said things that were "quotable," as in "There's a mouse loose in the room. Could it be in someone's sneakers?" and "Give me that book. These children deserve to read freely!"

This may seem hokey. It may even seem sort of crazy. You can absolutely come up with better plans! You just want a small, sudden, observable drama. What you will find is that staging a confrontation works because the suddenness of the altercation hooks the kids right away. You needn't stage an altercation, of course. You can catch one. School yards and lunch rooms are full of mini-dramas every day.

Channel students to write about the incident.

All of this is a drumroll leading up to the fact that you then announce to your kids that as writers, when things happen, they need to think, "I can write about this." Tell them that in instances like this, they can write a news story on what just happened. With a sense of urgency, say, "Open up your notebooks. You have five minutes to write down what you just witnessed." This work needs to be very quick and intense.

To scaffold your more struggling writers, you might say something like, "I, for instance, am thinking my news report could start, 'Today at 8:55 A.M., children in room 506 were startled to see . . .'" If you use a journalistic tone, including third person and a sense of specificity and drama, kids usually pick that tone up right away.

After a few minutes of writing, you might ask students to share with a partner. You might also read aloud some of their reports, telling the class to listen for things other "journalists" did that they feel worked well. They'll usually notice that when people wrote dramatically, this drew in readers. They will appreciate the use of detail, and they'll notice if some of the writing sounded like a news report. This entire endeavor can take just a few minutes if you keep the pace brisk: three minutes for the simulation, five minutes to write, ten minutes to share with partners and the whole class. All of this, of course, would depart from the usual minilesson template. Breaking stride is a good thing from time to time.

You may want to extend this early work. If so, you might ask your students to imagine that a newspaper is going to publish their reports, but only their first twenty-five words will be published. Therefore, they need to make those first twenty-five words count. They can change the words any way they want or delete some and use other words from later in their story. Give them five minutes to revise just the first twenty-five words, suggesting they aim for more specificity, detail, and/or drama. You will probably want to write these on a chart under the heading "Qualities of Strong News Reports."

Then let them get right to it, heads down, doing immediate revision. Ask them to share again with a partner and then at their tables. They could simply read aloud some of the lines they've written that they especially like. It's amazing how, in one day of writing, they'll have learned to observe closely, write quickly, and immediately revise! Their second versions will be better, especially since they only have to work on the first part of the story. They may add a title, and when you teach them to do this, you will be teaching a bit about angle or perspective. Typical titles might include "Kids Jump on Desks," "Fifth-Grader Traps Mouse on the Run," "Mouse Seeks Freedom," and so on. You could finish your lesson by starting a word chart of technical and academic words that relate to news reporters, such as *witness*, *this reporter*, *incident*, *bystander*, and *quoted*. You'll keep adding to this list over the course of the unit. Eventually you'll also start a second chart of vivid words: *shocked*, *bolted*, *surprised*, *dismayed*, *perplexed*.

Channel students to gather notes and generate entries.

That first day is intense and fast-paced, and it will set the tone for the kind of writing children will be doing this month. The next day, your more usual unit of study can begin. Probably the first thing you'll want to teach your young reporters is to generate stories from the world around them. You might recruit students to ponder the questions "What is news?" "What is newsworthy?" To support this inquiry, you might display several different kinds of news stories and help the class study these to decide what stories make the news. Youngsters can be helped to notice that news must be current: if it's new, it's news. Without taking long to do this, you can help students notice the diversity of issues and subjects that are covered by stories so that children realize that news covers famous people, big events, sports matches, the weather, and all sorts of human interest stories. Explain that events are newsworthy if they affect a wide range of people and more so if they're close to home and relevant to the population that is reading about them. If you ever needed to drive home that point, you could show children local as well as global news. The former will feel more accessible to children. The school's annual fundraiser will be easier to cover, for example, than the war in Afghanistan.

Of course, you don't want to cancel students' writing to study journalism. In any unit of study, children need to be writing almost every day for at least half an hour. So if you engage in a bit of a study about journalism, keep in mind that you can do some of this work side by side with the process of generating stories.

For children to be writing up a storm in this unit, you'll need to help them know that there are topics all around, ready to be harvested. Demand that children seek out and report on the stories in the world around them. Did they witness an injustice being committed in the hallway? An argument in the boys' bathroom? A commotion on the playground? An adventure during science lab? A scuffle on the bus? The Pulitzer Prize–winning journalist Donald Murray describes the journalist's job, as "writing with information," which requires paying attention to the world and asking the questions "What is, what isn't, what should be? What's going on and what does it mean?" Talk to your journalists about becoming a fly on the wall—observing, listening, taking furtive notes.

You will certainly want your students to be recording entries, and you can decide whether these are in their writer's notebooks or whether you want to create portable writer's notepads for the occasion. There are two reasons to invent portable notepads. First, these can later be deconstructed and taped into the writer's notebooks (which therefore also allows the notebooks to stay alive). Then, too, the portable notepads can help journalists assume new roles and walk into the new parts. But it is also possible for children to dust off their writer's notebooks and to use this unit to give those notebooks more life.

Whatever the writing tool may be, you will want to encourage your students to go around the school, looking for incidents that could become the center of a news story. "The best reporters are not born in the middle of war, riots, or conflict. They don't just happen to be passing by as world-changing events explode conveniently right before their eyes," you might tell children. "The best journalists seek out the action, positioning themselves in the spots where news is likely to occur." Explain that news stories are born, for example, when a reporter notices an act of heroism or an injustice, reads something on the bulletin board, or overhears the talk near the lockers. Encourage your reporters to seek out the hotspots of action, in school and out, gathering fodder for stories. If you have writing workshop at a time when your students can visit these sites, take the children with you, notes in hand, and have them come back and write a quick news report, not more than maybe 150 words long. You'll want to have them write several quick stories of this nature—providing time for writing—and then promptly sending them off to the "world" to collect more stories. You can also make "journalists' passes" so students have permission to disperse to other spaces in the school to do this.

Because you'll need your reporters to collect enough information to actually write the story, you'll teach them to take comprehensive notes. "Once they sniff out the makings of a newsworthy story, reporters investigate its details," you might teach. Journalism's conventional formula for getting complete information on a news story involves answering the five Ws and one H.

- What happened?
- Who was involved?
- When did it occur?
- Where did it all take place?

- Why did it happen?

- How did it happen?

That's actually a lot of information. The five Ws and H actually reflect good old-fashioned common sense that is as relevant and crucial to teach today as it ever was. Once you hold children accountable to answering this list of questions in their stories, you'll see that this is far from simple. Your reporters will need practice—and they'll benefit from studying mentor texts. You may start by modeling how to identify the five Ws and H answered in the headlines and leads of several mentor news stories until students can pick these out quickly and independently. Have partnerships support each other in this work. Midway through their writing, you might encourage partners to swap stories and find answers to the five Ws and H in each other's stories.

As writers create and gather investigative notes, remind them of Roy Peter Clark's advice from *Writing Tools*: don't return to the writing desk without the "name of the dog." In other words, teach reporters to procure specific details that will help make the story come to life for readers. If their story is about the healthier cafeteria menu, for example, it is helpful to mention that a sleek bottle of balsamic vinaigrette now stands in the spot that used to house the mayo tub. If the story is about an after-school skateboarding contest, a mention of the orange flame streaking across a purple board will help bring the story to life. Urge them to collect a quote—the direct words that somebody said—and to jot these with accuracy, along with the source.

Coach your reporters into producing three to four small news stories in this beginning bend and accept that these will be far from perfect. At this point, you will want your reporters to practice finding a newsworthy event to write about, to gather information on this, and to put it down on paper. Don't balk at the prospect of rushing students through this process. Issue deadlines, by all means. They are an essential element of journalism. In *Writing to Deadline*, Donald Murray shares on this topic: "When I give talks, people ask, 'How do you get the writing done?' My answer, 'I have a deadline.' But they ask, 'How do you know a piece of writing is finished?' 'When I get to the deadline.'" Murray goes on to describe how, early on in his career as a journalist, he wrote dozens of stories to deadline during his eight-hour shift, describing it as intensive training. You can think of this bend as intensive training in the art of generating news stories for your students. Practice, not perfection, is the aim of training.

Once youngsters have completed three to four quick cycles of gathering notes on a newsworthy event and fashioned these into rudimentary stories, you'll slow this pace and bring up the level of their news report writing skills by teaching them to revise. As they look over their stories to revise, you'll want to tuck in teaching that helps them learn the journalist's craft.

BEND II: REVISE NEWS STORIES FOR STRUCTURE AND TONE

Journalism is an increasingly wide field of writing, and there are many places to begin when teaching the journalist's craft. It makes sense, however, to start with structure. Because the technique, structure, style, and purpose of journalism are distinct from other forms of informational writing, children will need explicit instruction on how news reports are put together.

Teach students to craft a lead.

"A news report is like an upside-down pyramid," you might say, drawing this basic shape to explain. "The entire lot of basic information comes first," you'll say, pointing to the widest, top part of the inverted pyramid. Explain that journalists position the most substantial, interesting, and crucial information at the very start of the story so that the reader's most basic questions are answered within the very first sentence or two. Unlike fiction, the "lead" of a news story cannot afford to tantalize the reader with the promise of a mystery or entertain with witty dialogue; instead, it must provide hard facts with lucid briskness. You might begin this bend on "craft" by asking reporters to look back over the stories they generated in the first bend and to revise the leads to those stories. Share several mentor texts and point out that all the five Ws are usually answered within the headline and the first sentence or two. You might even lift several good news leads from various newspapers and post these around the room as examples, urging students to identify the specific information provided. Set your reporters up to mimic this top-heavy structure that presents the biggest and most important information first. That is, teach them to revise the leads to their news stories so they position the answers to the five Ws within their very first sentence.

Demonstrating this process will be invaluable. You might take a collected class experience and develop the lead of a news report from it, for example, "Students at P.S. 4 were shocked this Monday morning to find that a mouse had gotten loose in their classroom."

Point out that a simple, single sentence, like the one above, can provide the reader with immediate information on who, where, when, and what. Draw students' attention to the fact that a news story is not necessarily written in the chronology of how an event occurred. Unlike a story, it does not begin, "The day dawned bright and beautiful. Not a cloud in the sky, and the creek next to the factory bubbled cheerily. There was no warning that aggressive rioting would disrupt the streets by noon." Instead, a news report begins straight from the time, scene, and reasons of the big news itself: "Student riots rocked the campus of Wiley University, starting Friday after the last classes, protesting against . . ." News stories give the reader the big information first. There is no build-up to a climax, unlike texts with typical narrative structures.

Guide students as they move down the remainder of the inverted pyramid.

You'll go on to teach students that this lead is usually followed by a more detailed description of the event, supported by background information. This often includes a narration of the sequence in which something happened, pointing out what happened first, what happened next, and so on. You'll encourage your reporters to revise by adding details of what affected people or witnesses said, for example:

"I am outraged," said one parent. "My daughter could have been bitten."

Explain that reporters strive for balance, doing their best to cover two sides of every story. One way to do this is to document what a variety of witnesses said or felt—or what two different sides feel about an incident. To the above quote, therefore, a reporter might add:

Some students, however, expressed concern for the safety of the mouse. "It is a harmless enough creature and has as much right to life as any of us," declared one concerned fifth-grader. "I hope this doesn't bring out the traps and the poison."

You will want to help students note the use of the word *however* in the sentence above, explaining that a reporter will often say, "Some people think this . . . However, others think this . . ." Remind children to use a news reporter's tone, using people's full names when writing about them and referring to them by their last names if they are referred to again in the same piece. Since this is revision work and your reporters are no longer at the "scene" (time and place) of the actual story, they may not have all the ready-made quotes or details at their disposal; you can bend the rules and allow them to invent these if needed.

You'll also want to help students revise the endings to their news stories. You'll explain that the inverted pyramid often ends with the least crucial information—usually with conjectures made by a witness, by an authority, or by reporters themselves. These conjectures or guesses sometimes detail the possible effects that an event might have on neighbors or on the future or what follow-up courses of action might be. For example:

A thorough investigation by the Department of Health is likely to be conducted.

Or

Science classes will go on as usual in Room 107, but no student is likely to forget the furry little visitor.

During the revision process, you will also want to draw reporters' attention to consider the tone of news reports, explaining that this tone is different from the tone used in a memoir or a story. Read aloud a few news reports and ask students to note the use of the "outsider" third person, the officiousness with which facts are reported with accuracy and specificity. You could download a video clip if you want, anything from the famous eye-witness reporting of the *Hindenburg* to a news clip or a sports clip from the night before. Help your students talk about the tone of the pieces, the role of the reporter, the audience, the rapidity with which information is conveyed, and any language they notice.

Finally, draw students' attention to language. The best news stories are concise, to the point. They don't waste words. Demonstrate how long-winded writing can be tightened, how excess words can be lopped off to crystallize meaning, and how a single precise word can replace a phrase. Share news stories in which the journalist has practiced showing, not telling, and make clear that the best news stories contain only those carefully selected details that will evoke a strong sensory reaction in the reader.

The revisions your reporters make to their existing stories should take no more than three or four days, especially since news reports are shorter than many other kinds of writing. You'll want to keep your writers moving, engaged, and challenged by new tasks, moving them along to the next bend.

BEND III: CYCLE WITH PURPOSE THROUGH A JOURNALIST'S PROCESS

If you've ever tried your hand at an ice cream cranking machine, you'll have noted that the first cycle is always hardest—that the more cycles you crank through, the quicker and easier they become. This is true of everything, including cycling through a new kind of writing. Your news reporters have come full cycle, from generating a news story, gathering information for it, crafting a lead that answers the five Ws, inserting dialogue, and finally, structuring it through to a logical end. Now is the time to let them have another go—expecting that their process will be easier, smoother, and more purposeful. In this bend, you'll send them off to find and report on more news.

Some teachers have structured their workshops like actual newsrooms, with students assigned to various topics or parts of the school. For instance, some students may be in charge of stories in the lunchroom, others are in charge of bulletins from the main office, others might report from behind the scenes in the after-school parking lot, and so forth. Turning students into experts on one division of the school will increase their investment in their reporting.

Teach students how to conduct and incorporate interviews.

This time, you can set your reporters up to be more purposeful from the start. You might teach them to interview a witness or key player in the news that they are reporting. Your students will see that interviews provide more than just some quotes. They also provide important content for the story itself. Teach a simple interview protocol where you model how the reporter establishes a rapport or connection, asks a few preliminary questions, listens carefully for interesting ideas, asks follow-up questions, or says, "Say more about that," and elicits specific examples. You might want to conduct some role-playing scenarios with the children so they can practice interviews. Coach them in their body language, their note-taking, and their listening skills. You might conduct a mock interview of a colleague to demonstrate and also have students interview each other to practice. Explain that reporters take care to preserve the direct words of their interviewee to retain accuracy and authentic quotes for their news story. For this reason, reporters take along a small voice-recorder or practice speedy note-taking in shorthand. They may want to bring a partner to help with note-taking when they interview.

"Journalists prepare for interviews." This is important teaching. Students will not necessarily do this unless you prompt them to, and it can dramatically alter the results. Urge students to plan some specific questions to ask, to approach the interview with these questions in hand, and even to anticipate answers and prepare some follow-up questions for the most obvious answers. As they practice interviewing each other in class, make sure they listen carefully to their partners and ask questions that extend or clarify the answers that they receive.

You'll want your reporters to get multiple perspectives on a story so that they learn "balanced" reporting. You might even insist that they conduct more than one interview—that they get more than just one voice represented in their story. So they will interview the shopkeeper as well as the customer, the superintendent and the teacher as well as the student. When they return to their writing desks, demonstrate how to incorporate these direct quotes in a way that strengthens the story. "You don't just reproduce the entire interview verbatim, nor do you put in quote upon quote," you'll teach. You'll want to explain, "Journalists are selective in what they pick to quote. Usually these are the most provocative ideas or the ones that will stir the readers' imagination. They use only the best quotes."

Support students as they craft the news story.

Your journalists already have practice in presenting information hierarchically in the inverted pyramid. This time around, they will draft a purposeful lead that not only presents the most important information head on but also grabs readers' attention. Explain that a good lead—spelled *lede* in journalism—is always written in the active voice. For example, instead of the passive sentence "Students were stunned by a mouse scurrying across . . ." the active lede would read, "Mouse stuns students . . ." Similarly, "Experiments were conducted by scientists to . . ." is a passive sentence and needs to be converted to an active lead: "Scientists conducted experiments to . . ." You'll need to let students practice converting passive sentences into active ones, and set partners to check out each other's leads for passive weakness!

Similarly, help students craft an ending that provides an element of closure. Granted, the inverted pyramid suggests that the least important information is contained in the ending, but this does not mean that the ending can be shoddy and poorly developed. Instead, a thought-provoking ending leaves the reader thinking more about the news. To decide what to put in an ending, journalists might ask, "What background and technical details might the reader need?" You might ask students to look at the endings of several news stories that they've studied in the past month and notice what purpose these endings serve and mimic this in their own writing. Explain that there is nothing more frustrating for the reader than finishing a story with unanswered questions still hanging—that the journalist ensures that he or she has covered all sides and angles before ending.

Crafting an effective headline is part of journalism. The headline is more than a harbinger for the story that follows. It actually has a marketing angle too. "Read it here!" news headlines seem to yell. "You won't believe what just happened in our world. Read on." Ask students to collect a few headlines and study what is similar in many of them, how they are structured, and their economical use of words. In particular, draw students' attention to the use of strong verbs in each headline. You'll urge students to craft similar headlines for their own stories, headlines that hook the reader with concise, strong words. Explain that shorter headlines can have more impact than longer ones, and demonstrate how a longer headline might be shortened to the bare minimum of words possible.

In this bend, you'll want students to generate only one or two stories but to craft these with purpose and revise them into perfection until they feel ready for publication in the upcoming bend.

BEND IV: EDIT AND PUBLISH

The relationship between the journalist and the editor is an interesting one. A newspaper editor is a task-master, writing critic, and advisor rolled into one. You might have your journalists become each other's editors and ask them to check each other's writing for the correct use of conventions, paragraphing, and the inverted pyramid structure and to try to answer the five Ws and H within the headline and lead. You might have small groups come together to polish their headlines and arrange their stories together to create mini-newspapers to share around the school.

To bring this process to life, you might even allow students to create cartoons or illustrations or to insert photographs to include in their newspaper. If you have time, you might talk a little about photojournalism and how each photograph in a newspaper supports the story in answering the five Ws and H. Again, mentor photos and illustrations in actual newspapers will play an invaluable role. Celebrate these newspapers by displaying them in a prominent place for the world to admire.

Fantasy

RATIONALE/INTRODUCTION

Welcome to the fantastic world of heroes, dragons, wizards, and spells! This unit has the capacity to become a transformative unit, one where students are able to synthesize many of the writing skills they have been honing all year, as well as push themselves past their comfort zones into new areas of growth. The key is knowing that this unit is a wolf in sheep's clothing—meaning that you are reteaching narrative writing with a very different package.

Your students will presumably have written narratives either earlier this year or in fourth grade. It benefits writers enormously to have an opportunity to return to a form or genre; students will have greater control when they return to a genre, and they will use familiar strategies with greater finesse to accomplish new and bigger goals. This return to the narrative genre also gives students an opportunity to tackle the Common Core's significant expectations for students in both writing and reading. The CCSS highlight the fact that students need to be able to talk and think about the reasons that authors make specific craft moves—shifting perspective, using symbolism and metaphor, for example—and there is no better way to understand authorial intent than to have one's own experience deliberately using craft moves to highlight specific meanings.

If your students happen to be engaged in fantasy reading while they are also writing fantasies, you can teach them that writers read with a special lens, noticing writing craft. Writers will want to try some of the craft moves they notice in the fantasy novels they love—the description of fantastical worlds, the insertion of magical objects or characters, the use of symbolism to guide the reader toward interpretations, and so forth. Students will be able to do this work as writers especially if they have been reading fantasy novels with an eye toward the decisions that authors have made and the connections between those decisions and the meanings in the stories. Readers can learn to notice moments that provoke a strong emotional response and to think about why the author may have written those moments in that way and about how those moments connect to the whole of the text. Then during the writing unit of study, students can create their own such moments.

This unit is a great joy to teach, and it is also a tremendous challenge. The power and the challenge of the genre relate to the fact that students love to write fantasy and think of it as the easiest genre to write because they believe (mistakenly) that anything goes. They are apt to throw in magical characters, worlds, even multiple plotlines with armies from warring nations doing battle. Almost anything they have ever read or seen in movies will land in the same muddied piece. Of course, you'll want to embrace your students' passion for fantasy writing, but meanwhile, you will also need to be a strong, decisive leader throughout the unit, exerting more than the usual amount of influence. Unless you are firm and clear, students will quickly become utterly mired in drafts that are so rich, long, and problematic that it will be hard for you to know how to help students lift the level of those pieces. On the other hand, because students have such energy to bring to this unit, if you teach with clarity and power, students will match your power with their own, and the result can be a powerful form of deeply engaged learning.

This unit requires that students bring a background in narrative writing and, ideally, in fiction. Your students will have worked in personal narrative writing earlier this year, and you may have decided to also teach them a unit on fiction or historical fiction writing prior to this unit. Their prior experience with narrative writing will be an important precursor to this unit. Above all, it will be important that students enter this unit knowing how to show, not tell, and how to write in scenes rather than in summaries.

MANDATES, TESTS, STANDARDS

Before you officially launch the unit, you will presumably want to do a quick on-demand writing assessment. You can either use the generic narrative prompt or you can alter it so that you are inviting students to essentially flash-draft a fantasy piece. If you decide to do the latter, you might say to your students, "Our next unit is going to be fantasy, and I would love to know what you already know about writing fantasy stories. Would you please write a scene or two of a fantasy story, including everything you know about writing strong narratives and everything you know about fantasy?" Whether you channel students specifically toward fantasy or simply invite them to write a narrative, either way, your students will have one period to do this. You can then review what they have written with an eye first and foremost for what they know or are approximating in narrative writing. The fifth-grade narrative checklist can be an important tool, helping you to contrast what students are able to do with the expectations for fifth-graders. As you review this writing, you will also see what your students already know about how fantasy writing should go. Prepare to be surprised! Students often know more than teachers do about this genre, and many a teacher finds herself furiously revising her unit plans after seeing all that her students already know and can do.

A SUMMARY OF THE BENDS IN THE ROAD FOR THIS UNIT

We recommend that students cycle through the process of planning, drafting, and revising a fantasy story twice during this unit. During their second round through the process, your writers will make choices with greater independence, confidence, and productivity.

To leave time for students to get to another round of writing, it is best to shepherd them fairly quickly through generating seed ideas and rehearsing for drafting. When students spend weeks and weeks rehearsing, the volume of writing they do plummets significantly.

In Bend I (Collect Ideas for Fantasy Fiction and Develop a Story with Depth, Significance, and Believability), your students will spend a week or so writing entries in notebooks, producing at least a page and a half to two pages of writing at school and another page and a half at home. You'll teach your writers to raise the level of their writing as they collect entries and eventually to select one of them as a seed idea. Your writers will spend just one or two days rehearsing this idea, trying out various methods of planning, and finally making a commitment to one plan.

In Bend II (Draft and Revise: Craft a Compelling Fantasy Fiction Story), you will channel your writers to spend an intense day (or possibly two) fast-drafting their fantasy stories. Right away, you will begin teaching revision moves that can be used to raise the quality of drafts for those who are still composing or to make significant changes for those who are ready to do so. The revision work students will do in this bend is drawn from some of the most crucial narrative work: showing not telling, stretching out the heart of the story, and bringing out deeper meaning through dialogue, actions, and internal thinking. At the end of this bend, you will teach a few editing strategies, as well as provide students the opportunity to do some self-reflection and goal-setting using the Narrative Writing Checklists.

In Bend III (Develop, Draft, and Revise a Second Fantasy Short Story), you will set your students up to cycle through the writing process once again, this time transferring all they have learned to a second piece of writing. You will teach your writers to mentor themselves using published fantasies, ideally ones that are short.

In Bend IV (Edit and Publish: Prepare the Fantasy Story for Readers), students will choose just one piece to edit and publish. They will spend a day or two revising their stories, perhaps with an eye toward bringing out a theme or a message. Then, you will teach some targeted editing moves based on your assessment of students' writing. Finally, you will provide the opportunity for your fifth-graders to publish and celebrate their hard work.

GETTING READY
Gather Materials for Students

As mentioned earlier, many teachers have found that this unit pairs well with a reading workshop unit on fantasy reading. It can be most supportive to begin the reading unit a week or two in advance of the writing unit, so that students are immersed in the genre before they attempt to write fantasy. The fantasy that students read, however, will tend to be full-length novels, and it is critical for you to remember that they will be writing short stories. Novels and films give students the idea that the only great ideas for fantasy stories are those of the epic variety. A great way to combat this is to offer students experiences with brief fantasy stories—picture books and short stories—that are more accessible. Some of our favorite fantasy mentor texts include picture books such as *Merlin and the Dragons, Stranger in the Mirror, Raising Dragons,* and *The Rainbabies*, as well as short stories from anthologies such as *Fire and Wings, But That's Another Story,* or *A Glory of Unicorns*. Some of these texts will be more appropriate for middle school students than for fifth-graders, so select your mentor text with care.

While you are gathering materials, we also suggest you consider creating a small basket of photographs, geologic guides, and nonfiction books on animals and the environment. Jane Yolen has helped us remember that students need to know that fantasy writers must either be keen observers of the world or they must be avid researchers or both. Yolen writes, "All the fantasy authors I know research volumes on wildlife, wildflowers, insects, and birds." These kinds of resources will help students to bring some realism into their fantasy—or at least keep their fantasy grounded in the believable (as odd as that may sound!). You might also consider other resources, such as baby name books (to help students choose names with meaning, significance, and history behind them) and dictionaries (which can be helpful when looking up the etymology of words). Another favorite book, and one you will want to have on the shelf with easy access for students and teacher alike is Gail Carson Levine's *Writing Magic*—a book she has written for children about writing fantasy. When choosing resources, it's helpful to remember that although fantasy writing weaves a world of make-believe, it is based (often meticulously) on reality.

BEND I: COLLECT IDEAS FOR FANTASY FICTION AND DEVELOP A STORY WITH DEPTH, SIGNIFICANCE, AND BELIEVABILITY

Sir Max Beerbohm once said, "All fantasy should have a solid base in reality." This notion often comes as a shock to novice fantasy writers. Isn't fantasy all about making everything up? Anything goes? In fact, most fantasy is allegorical—real-life stories and lessons cloaked in fantasy settings, characters, quests, or all of the above. When we teach students to collect ideas for fantasy stories, we do ourselves and our students a favor when we follow two simple guidelines: keep fantasy stories grounded in some way in the real world and move *quickly* through the collecting section of this unit. Both of these guidelines help keep students' ideas in the realm of bite-sized, approachable possibilities.

Inspire writers to gather ideas based on one's life, different settings, or ideas that matter.

With this in mind, almost any ideas that worked with realistic fiction idea gathering can be recast and used in this unit. You might teach students that they can look at their own lives and imagine how events and issues could be turned into fantasy stories. A student with a sick parent might create a fantasy story where the hero must go on a quest to find the magical potion to save the ailing queen, for example.

You could teach students to consider settings as another place to develop possible story ideas. These settings can be in our world (what would happen if Bobby was sitting in math class and an elf popped out of his pencil case?), built upon portals to another world (Bobby opens his backpack to find himself transported into a castle made entirely of school supplies.), or else entirely in a fantasy world (Robert lives in a thatched cottage in a village where everyone rides unicorns.). Students can then use these settings to imagine possible story ideas and even characters that might inhabit these settings.

Additionally, you might have students revisit their notebooks, particularly their memoir or essay work, to see what life ideas matter most to them. Big world ideas and issues can be particularly potent sources of inspiration in an allegorical genre, and fantasy stories can carry messages such as "You don't need to succumb to peer pressure to be accepted" and "When the going gets tough, the tough get going." You can teach students to think of possible fantasy story ideas that build off ideas that matter to them. For example, if a student is passionate about the environment, she might craft a story idea that revolves around a magical forest that is being pillaged for its magical plants by an evil dragon and slowly dying. A young peasant girl must slay the dragon to spare the forest.

Early in the unit, we recommend that story ideas are collected as story blurbs—not as a list of possible story ideas, each captured in a line, but rather as a collection of short summaries that capture how a story might go, including possible main characters, the problem, and several possible resolutions. We, of course, are fully expecting that the ideas students ultimately choose will continue to morph and develop throughout the writing process, but it is essential that students approach their writing with well-formed ideas for ways their stories might unfold.

In the gathering stage, you will want to give very clear feedback to students. This is your opportunity to cut some of those epic and novel-length story ideas off at the pass! Teach whole-class and small-group sessions that channel students to write single-arc story lines. Because your students will be writing short stories, it is also important that their stories contain only one or two main characters and only a couple of obstacles, rather than a never-ending series of obstacles. In other words, when a student wants to write a story about a prince who might lose his kingdom if he does not go to war with another kingdom, and if that student wants to summarize twenty years of battles, magicians, and quests that occur before the hero finally regains his crown, you will encourage that student to choose one or two episodes from that epic storyline. Perhaps in the end, the whole story will revolve around the one day when the boy won the crown in a moment of magical valor.

Encourage writers to explore story ideas in their notebooks.

Another word of caution here: many students will want to leap with both feet into drafting their stories in their notebooks rather than collecting several ideas to choose from. This can only lead to thin stories, heavy on plot, light on craft and structure, and almost always too exhaustively long to revise. You will want to be strong on this front and encourage students to draft and revise, to weigh and reject, a few ideas before committing to one. The notebook is a great place to explore lots of different ideas before settling on one. You might find it simplest to pull out old charts you have from previous units that instruct students in the fine art of generating lots of story ideas. Or you might opt to add to their repertoire of idea-generating strategies. You might teach students that some fantasy writers choose their story ideas based on the messages they want to send out into the world.

Once students have chosen their story ideas, you will want them to spend a day developing aspects of those ideas. For example, you might suggest they flesh out an idea by writing long about the settings. They might also want to develop their main characters (or heroes) using some of the strategies they learned in the fourth-grade realistic fiction unit, *The Arc of Story: Writing Realistic Fiction*, if they were part of the fourth-grade Units of Study curriculum.

We recommend that you encourage students to recycle a planning strategy they used with some success earlier in the year: your students may have planned narratives using story booklets or using timelines or using story arcs. The important caveat is this: in classrooms that have had a high degree of success with this unit, teachers have told students their story ideas must be comprised of two or three well-developed scenes only. This admonition, we find, channels students away from writing complicated, epic narratives.

If you want to give a fantastical bent to the topic of ways to generate story ideas, you could always show one of your fantasy mentor texts, such as "Family Monster" from *But That's Another Story*. As students review the mentor text, give them some tips. Help them to see, for example, that if there's to be magic in a story, it needs to be introduced at the beginning of the story to make it more believable. You might also teach your more advanced writers that it can help to do a double-decker plan for a story, including one line for plot points and the other line for the deeper meaning or internal story line or the character's learning journey (CCSS W.5.3.a).

BEND II: DRAFT AND REVISE: CRAFT A COMPELLING FANTASY FICTION STORY

You will want students to move rather quickly through drafting and into the revision process, both because otherwise students can get bogged down in epic story creation and also because most writers find that drafts are best if they are written fast and furious. So, it is our suggestion that you plan to teach only one (perhaps two) drafting minilessons, moving quickly to revision so that students use revision as a time to work toward incorporating the qualities of good writing into their text.

Aside from reminding your students of all the great narrative writing strategies they've learned and used all year by pulling out and referring to past charts and possibly even past writing pieces, you will want to teach students that the best way to write the strongest drafts is to get lost in writing their drafts, much as people get lost in books that they're reading. You can suggest to your students, "You know what it is like when you miss the call for dinner because you're so engrossed in a good book? Or you don't hear the call to the share meeting because you are so engrossed in a book? Well, that sort of absorption is what a writer feels when writing a fantasy story."

Channel students to focus their imagination and draft quickly.

You will want to teach students that by focusing their imaginations, by either closing their eyes and picturing or else perhaps story-telling to a partner before they write, they can get themselves imagining all the sights, sounds, and even smells of that place. Writing will be powerful if students make the story they are writing feel as concrete and *real* as possible (CCSS W.5.3.d).

Of course, once a draft is written—quickly—you'll want to remind your students that all serious writers revise. Of course, the possibilities for revision are endless, in part because the students are often so invested in their fantasy stories that they are willing to try more and work harder. There are dizzying teaching opportunities here! You will, of course, want to be a close observer of your students' drafts to assess what your students are most ready to learn as well as what they most need to learn. The Narrative Writing Checklist and the Common Core State Standards will be helpful guides in this work.

Teach students to revise and edit with a few key strategies.

A favorite revision teaching point for many teachers in this unit is to teach students how to make their readers suspend disbelief. One way to do this is by teaching students that the more specific they are in their descriptions about key characters, settings, and even objects, the more believable these things become. For example, if a writer wants to talk about a table that begins to float, one way to make that unbelievable concept more believable is to describe it in great and concrete detail, so that "The table floated across the room" becomes, "The round cherry wood table with seventeen pieces of gum stuck to its underside, suddenly began to vibrate under their fingers. Lyssa watched in shock as her marble composition notebook slid off its shiny surface as it rose one foot and then two feet off the library's sensible linoleum floor." Then, too, magic is more believable if it doesn't come as a surprise. For example, if we plan to have our hero use a magic stone to cast a protective spell, the first time we hear of this stone should not be when the dragon is about to breathe his fiery breath.

One of the most important revision moves is one you have been teaching all year long. You'll want to remind students that they need to develop meaning and significance in stories through showing and not telling. They will need you to remind them to write with a balance of action, thought, dialogue, and setting, letting their stories unfold bit by bit (CCSS W.5.3.b). You will have already taught them to stop, identify, and then stretch out the heart of the story—even going as far as using scissors and tape to elaborate on crucial moments in stories. This lesson will need to be taught all over again because many students get so lost in the fun of fantasy that their stories go on and on and on and on. There is no theme, no coherent shape, and no heart of the story. Of course, once students are clear about the real meanings they hope to convey, they can learn to make their settings and objects into symbols of deeper meanings in stories. The magic stone can come to represent the bravery the heroine must show, despite her fears. It is tiny, but strong—just as our heroine is. The dark night can stand for the fear the heroine is grappling with before the dawn comes.

A word on editing: don't wait until your students are fancying up their pieces for publication to remind them to hold themselves accountable to check for proper punctuation, capitalization, and spelling. Even first drafts should incorporate punctuation, paragraphs, and correct spelling of high-frequency words. Additionally, if you teach a few key punctuation moves, you will be able to help writers attempt higher levels of sophistication in their writing. For example, you might teach your students that characters in fantasy fiction often refer to conversations they had in the past. Then, show how writers punctuate a quote within a quote, when one character is quoting another, with single quotation marks.

As you wrap up this bend, and your students wrap up their first fantasy story, take one session to channel students toward some reflection and goal-setting. Ask students to study their work with the narrative checklist in hand and to take a brave critical stance as they do this. Then, give students some time to make revisions to their drafts based on what they noticed and to set some goals for their future work.

BEND III: DEVELOP, DRAFT, AND REVISE A SECOND FANTASY SHORT STORY

In this bend, you will channel your fifth-graders to cycle through the process of gathering ideas, choosing a seed idea, and developing, drafting, and revising a second fantasy piece. Bring the anchor charts from the start of the unit to the easel and challenge students to use these charts and all that they have learned to plan their own progress through the writing process. Make sure they do rely upon the process, putting into motion all that you taught them earlier. During this bend, you can also ramp up expectations by leaning heavily on mentor texts, channeling your writers to read fantasy with a writer's eye, beginning with studying mentor texts to spark ideas for what to write about.

As your students return to their notebooks to collect story blurbs, remind them that their notebook work should reflect all they have learned about fantasy writing. Now, they should have a keener sense of what kinds of ideas would make a good fantasy story (in other words, those grounded in reality) and which ideas would be difficult to pull off. Then, channel them to choose a seed idea quickly and to lean on mentor texts as they rehearse and then draft.

If your students are reading fantasies while writing them, tap into this relationship. Students can bring their own stories into the reading workshop and read their own stories and each other's just as they read stories by published authors.

Demonstrate how writers study craft moves and language used by fantasy authors.

Students can study craft moves fantasy authors regularly employ. What can they notice about sentence length and variation? When do fantasy authors use longer or shorter sentences? (Hint: most authors use longer sentences when they are describing things or slowing action down and shorter sentences when there is action.) What do they notice about the author's use of dialogue? How does the author make different characters speak differently? Word choice? Punctuation? Speech habits? How do the fantasy stories that students love the most tend to start? How do they tend to end? All of these things can be studied and then emulated.

Finally, you might consider referring to books written by adult writers of fantasy for other professional writers. These books such as *How to Write Science Fiction and Fantasy*, by Orson Scott Card (2001); *The Complete Guide to Writing Fantasy, Vol. 1: Alchemy with Words*, by Darin Park and Tom Dullemond (2006); and "Living the Future" by Gardner Dozois, from *Writing Science Fiction and Fantasy* (1991), would not be books that would be directly approachable for children, but with an eye for the types of skills you want your students to learn, you can easily modify the strategies discussed in these books.

This is also a good time for kids to develop some "expert" vocabulary. Mysteries are full of words such as *perpetrator*, *investigator*, *red herring*, and so on. Historical fiction is full of historical terms such as *hearth*, *homestead*, and *pinafore*. Fantasy often has archaic, medieval words such as *saddlebags*, *abode*, and so on. Additionally, you might teach your writers that many fantasy authors use some Latin or Greek words, or other forms of etymology, to create new words for the creations of their imagination (CCSS L.5.4.b). Your writers can also create individual and shared word banks of the technical words they are collecting as they read, and they can weave these into their writing.

BEND IV: EDIT AND PUBLISH: PREPARE THE FANTASY STORY FOR READERS

In this bend, guide students to choose one of the stories they have written and to prepare it for publication. You may want to begin by doing some shared thinking about the final product the class will be creating. If you have decided to channel writers toward an anthology, you may want to hold a whole-class discussion about some of the themes and issues they are developing in their stories. Ask writers to think about connections between these themes and issues and to use these connections to choose a theme for the class anthology. Your class may notice that many of the stories deal with the idea that one can only become great by facing one's fears. Or many of the stories might tell of an underdog who comes out on top in the end. As a class, you may decide to develop two or three anthologies with different themes.

Once students have chosen a piece for publication, you might decide to have one final session on revision in which you channel writers to choose their own work, with a goal of really bringing out the theme in their stories.

Then, channel students toward some fairly rigorous editing work. You may want to begin by guiding students to study mentor texts for editing help. You can show students how to attend to the punctuation usage employed in longer sentences (commas, dashes, colons), as well the way fantasy writers choose to spell words—even made-up words—with conventional spelling in mind.

When students move to publishing, you might opt to have them publish their books as picture books, since so much of fantasy writing lends itself nicely to visuals. There are several kinds of celebrations that lend themselves beautifully to this unit. For example, you could have a "story hour," where your students read excerpts of their stories to a younger class. To add some drama, you might ask students to come to their publishing party dressed as one of the characters from their stories. That way, the younger classes can be read to by fairies, elves, wizards, and dragons! Alternatively, you might tap into your fifth-graders' flare for drama by giving them the opportunity to choose sections of their stories to act out for an audience of parents.

Part Two: Differentiating Instruction for Individuals and Small Groups: If . . . Then . . . Conferring Scenarios

THERE IS NO GREATER CHALLENGE, WHEN TEACHING WRITING, than to learn to confer well. And conferring well is a big deal. It matters. If you can pull your chair alongside a child, study what he or she has been doing, listen to the child's own plans, and then figure out a way to spur that youngster on to greater heights, that ability means that you will always be able to generate minilessons, mid-workshop teaching points, and share sessions that have real-world traction because these are really conferences-made-large.

However, knowing conferring matters doesn't make it easier to master. Even if you know that learning to confer well is important, even if you devote yourself to reading about the art of conferring, you are apt to feel ill-prepared for the challenges that you encounter.

I remember Alexandra, tall with long brown hair and a thick Russian accent. I'd pull up beside her after the minilesson, notebook in hand, ready to execute the perfect conference. We'd talk, I'd research, and without fail, every time, I'd be left with the same terrifying realization: "She's already doing everything! I don't know what to teach her." In an attempt to preserve my own integrity, I'd leave her with a compliment. Despite having joined our class mid-year, despite the challenge of mastering a new language and adapting to a new culture, Alexandra implemented anything and everything I hoped she would as a writer. I thought, "What should she do next?" I was stuck.

Then there was a child I'll call Matthew, who in truth, represents many others across my years as a teacher. It felt as if I was always conferring with him—modeling, pulling him into small groups, implementing all the scaffolds I knew of—and yet he didn't make the progress I hoped for. In reality, it felt like nothing worked. As I'd sit beside him, looking over his work, I couldn't help but wonder what was happening. Why was my teaching passing him over? What do I teach him, right now in this conference, when his writing needs *everything*?

If you have had conferences like these and end up wondering what's wrong, know that you aren't alone. Teachers across the world find that conferring well is a challenge. Most of us have, at one time or another, written questions on our hands, or on cue cards, that we want to remember to ask. Many of us have mantras that we repeat to ourselves, over and over. "Teach the writer, not the writing." "It's a good conference if the writer leaves, wanting to write." "Your job is to let this child teach you how to help."

Many of the books on conferring will help you understand the architecture of a conference. You'll learn to research first, then to compliment, then to give critical feedback and/or to teach. You'll learn tips about each part of a conference. When researching, follow more than one line of inquiry. If you ask "What are you working on?" and hear about the child's concerns with one part of the writing, don't jump to teaching that part of the writing until you generate a second line of inquiry—whether it's "What do you plan to do next?" or "How do you feel about this piece?" or "If you were going to revise this, what might you do?" There are similar tips that you'll learn about other aspects of conferring too.

But you will no doubt feel as if there is another kind of help that you need. You will probably want help knowing not only *how* to confer, but also knowing *what* to teach.

Visiting hundreds of schools has given me a unique perspective on that question, a perspective that may be difficult to come by when you are in one classroom, with one set of children with very particular needs.

After working in so many schools, with so many youngsters, I've begun to see patterns. I notice that when X is taught, children often need Y or Z. I meet one Matthew in Chicago and another in Tulsa, Oklahoma. I met Alexandras in Seattle and Shanghai. And I've begun to realize that, despite the uniqueness of each child, there are familiar ways they struggle and predictable ways in which a teacher can help with those struggles. Those ways of helping come from using all we know about learning progressions, writing craft, language development, and grade-specific standards to anticipate and plan for the individualized instruction that students are apt to need.

The charts that follow are designed to help you feel less empty-handed when you confer. I've anticipated some of the most common struggles you will see as you teach narrative, opinion, and information writing through the units of study in this series and I've named a bit about those struggles in the "If . . ." column of the charts. When you identify a child (or a group of children) who resembles the "If . . ." that I describe, then see if perhaps the strategy I suggest might help. That strategy is described in the column titled "After acknowledging what the child is doing well, you might say . . ." Of course, you will want to use your own language. What I've presented is just one way your teaching might go!

Often you will want to leave the writer with a tangible artifact of your work together. This will ensure that he or she remembers the strategy you've worked on and next time you meet with the child, it will allow you to look back and see what you taught the last time you worked together. It will be important for you to follow up on whatever the work is that you and the youngster decide upon together. Plan to check back in, asking a quick "How has the work we talked about been going for you? Can you show me where you've tried it?"

Some teachers choose to print the "Leave the writer with . . ." column onto reams of stickers or label paper (so they can be easily placed in students' notebooks). You also might choose to print them out on plain paper and tape them onto the writer's desk as a reminder (see the CD-ROM for this chart in reproducible format). I hope these charts will help you anticipate, spot, and teach into the challenges your writers face during the independent work portion of your writing workshop.

Narrative Writing

If …	After acknowledging what the child is doing well, you might say …	Leave the writer with …
Structure and Cohesion		
The story lacks focus. This writer has written a version of a "bed to bed" story, beginning with the start of a day or large event ("I woke up and had breakfast.") and progressing to the end ("I came home. It was a great day."). The event unfolds in a bit-by-bit fashion, with each part of the story receiving equal weight.	You are learning to write more and more, stretching your stories across tons of pages. That's great. But here's the new challenge. Writers need to be able to write a lot and still write a *focused* story. What I mean by this is that writers can write a whole story about an event that only lasted 20 minutes, and it can still be tons of pages long. To write a really fleshed out, well developed, small moment story, it is important to move more slowly through the sequence of the event, and capture the details on the page.	Not the whole trip, the whole day: 20 minutes!! Write with details. I said, I thought, I did.
The story is confusing or seems to be missing important information. This writer has written a story that leaves you lost, unable to picture the moment or understand the full sequence of events. She may have left out information regarding where she was or why something was happening, or may have switched suddenly to a new part of the story without alerting the reader.	I really want to understand this story, but it gets confusing for me. Will you remember that writers need to become readers and to reread their own writing, asking, "Does this make sense? Have I left anything out that my reader might need to know?" Sometimes it is helpful to ask a partner to read your story, as well, and to tell you when the story is making sense (thumbs up) and when it is confusing (thumbs down).	I reread my writing to make it clearer. I ask myself, "Does this make sense? Have I left anything out that my reader might need to know?" If I need to, I add more information or a part that is missing into the story.
The story has no tension. This writer's story is flat, without any sense of conflict or tension. The story is more of a chronicle than a story. If there is a problem, there is no build-up around possible solutions. Instead, the dog is simply lost and then found.	You told what happened in your story, in order, so I get it. But to make this into the kind of story that readers can't put down, the kind that readers read by flashlight in bed, you have to add what writers call edge-of-the-seat tension. Instead of just saying I did this, I did this, I did this, you need to have the narrator want something really badly and then run into difficulties, or trouble … so readers are thinking, "Will it work? Won't it?" You've got to get readers all wound up! Right now, reread and find the part of the story where you could show what the main character really wants.	Edge-of-the-seat tension: 1. Someone really wants something. 2. Someone encounters trouble. 3. Someone tries, tries, tries.

If ...	After acknowledging what the child is doing well, you might say ...	Leave the writer with ...
The story has no real or significant ending. This writer has ended her story in a way that feels disappointing to the reader. Occasionally this will be because she has left loose ends unresolved, but most often it is because the ending of the story has little to do with the significance of the story itself. The ending may be something like, "Then I went home," or "The End!" She needs help identifying what her story is really about and then crafting an ending that ties directly to that meaning.	Sometimes it seems like your endings just trail off, and they aren't as powerful as they could be because of that. Writers know that the ending of a story is the last thing with which a reader will be left. Today, I want to teach you one tip for writing an ending that is particularly powerful. Writers ask, "What is this story really about?" Once they have the answer to that, they decide on a bit of dialogue or internal thinking, a descriptive detail, or a small action that will end the story in a way that ties back to that meaning.	Writers end a story in a way that shows what the story is **really** about. They might do this by including: • Dialogue • Internal thinking • A descriptive detail • A small action that ties back to the true meaning behind the story
The writer is new to the writing workshop or this particular genre of writing. This writer struggles because narrative is a new genre for her. She may display certain skill sets (e.g., the ability to use beautifully descriptive language or literary devices) but lacks the vision of what she is being asked to produce. Her story is probably long and unfocused and is usually dominated by summary, not storytelling.	Someone famously once said, "You can't hit a target if you don't know what that target is." This is especially true for writers. They can't write well if they don't have a vision, a mental picture, of what they hope to produce. Today, I want to teach you that one way writers learn about the kinds of writing they hope to produce is by studying mentor texts. They read a mentor text once, enjoying it as a story. Then, they read it again, this time asking, "How does this kind of story seem to go?" They label what they notice and then try it in their own writing.	Writers use mentor texts to help them imagine what they hope to write. They: • Read the text and enjoy it as a good story. • Reread the text and ask, "How does this kind of story seem to go?" • Note what they notice. • Try to do some of what they noticed in their own writing.
The writer does not use paragraphs. This writer does not use paragraphs to separate the different parts of his story. Because of this, the story is difficult to read and hold onto. He needs support understanding the importance of paragraphs, as well as the various ways writers use them.	Your writing will be a thousand times easier to read when you start using paragraphs. A paragraph is like a signal to a reader. It says, "Halt! Take a tiny break. Do you understand what is happening so far? Okay, I'm going to keep going!" Paragraphs give your readers an opportunity to take in your stories, and they also alert readers to important things like scene changes and new dialogue. Today, I want to teach you a few of the ways writers use paragraphs. Writers use paragraphs when a new event is starting, when their story is switching to a new time or place, when a new character speaks, or to separate out an important part that needs space around it.	Make a New Paragraph Here: • Very important part that needs space around it • New event • New time • New place • New character speaks
Elaboration		
The writer has created a story that is sparse, with little elaboration. This writer has written a story that is short, with one or more parts that need elaboration. He has conveyed the main outline of an event (this happened, then this happened, then this happened), but there is no sense that he has expanded on any one particular part.	You have gotten skilled at telling what happens, in order, but you write with just the bare bones sequence. Like, if you went out for supper yesterday and I asked you, "How was your dinner at the restaurant?" and you answered, "I went to the restaurant. I ate food. It was good." That's not the best story, right? It is just the bare bones with no flesh on them—like a skeleton. Can you try to flesh out your story?	Not: I ate food. I came home. But: Details, details, details

If ...	After acknowledging what the child is doing well, you might say ...	Leave the writer with ...
The story is riddled with details. In an attempt to elaborate or make a story compelling, the writer has listed what seem to be an endless number of tangential details. ("I got on the ride. There were a lot of people there. I was wearing a bright red shirt with a little giraffe on it. I was eating funnel cake.") This sort of elaboration often makes the piece feel monotonous, as if there is no real purpose guiding the writer's choice of details.	Although you are great at including details, you actually choose too many details. Writers are choosy about the details they include in a story. They know they can't include every detail they remember, so they have to decide which parts of their story to stretch out with details and which parts to move through more quickly. Writers ask, "What is this story really about?" and then stretch out the part of the story that goes with that meaning. Then, they cut details from the parts that are less important.	Although it is great to write with details—some writers write with too many details. Writers need to decide which details to **keep** and which to **cut**. They: • Ask, "What is my story really about?" • Stretch out the heart of the story. • Shorten less important parts.
The story is swamped with dialogue. This writer is attempting to story-tell, not summarize, but is relying too heavily on dialogue to accomplish this mission. The story is full of endless dialogue ("Let's play at the park," I said. "Okay," Jill said. "Maybe we should play on the swings," I said. "I agree," Jill said. "Great!" I said.). This writer needs to learn that dialogue is an important part of storytelling but cannot be the only device a writer uses to move a story forward.	Sometimes, writers make their characters talk—and talk and talk and talk. Today, I want to teach you that writers use dialogue, but they use it sparingly. They make sure their writing has a balance of action and dialogue by alternating between the two and by cutting dialogue that does not give the reader important information about the character or the story.	Writers make sure that their writing has a balance of dialogue and action: • They often alternate between action and dialogue as they write. • They cut dialogue that does not give the reader important information about the character or story.
The writer has written the external story but not the internal story. This writer has captured the events of a story precisely, and likely has done a fine job of moving the story along at an appropriate pace. What is missing, however, is the internal story. That is, as each event occurs, the main character is merely swept along with the current of events ("'Don't you ever do that again!' my dad yelled. He wagged his finger at me. I went up to my room and sat down to do my homework.") and has little emotional response. The reader is left wondering what the main character is feeling and thinking throughout the story, and as a result, the story lacks a certain depth.	When we first learn to write stories, we learn to tell the events that happened. We tell what happened first, then next, then next. As we become strong writers, though, it's important not just to write the external story, but also to write the internal story. Today, I want to teach you that when planning for and drafting a story, the writer plans not just the actions, but also the character's *reactions* to the events.	Writers tell not just what happened in a story—the **actions**—but also how the character felt about each of those events—the **reactions**.

If …	After acknowledging what the child is doing well, you might say …	Leave the writer with …
The writer struggles to identify and convey a deeper meaning. This writer's story likely contains most of the surface elements you are looking for but seems to lack a sense of purpose. When asked why she is writing this particular piece or what she hopes to convey to her reader, she struggles to find an answer. Because of this, each part of the story is often given equal attention, without any one part having been elaborated on. Dialogue, details, and other forms of narrative craft are used to move the story forward but do not contribute to the reader's understanding of the meaning or theme.	Everybody has stories to tell. At a certain point in your life as a writer, knowing *why* you want to tell these stories becomes almost as important as writing them. What I mean by this, and what I want to teach you today, is that writers reflect on the moments of their lives and ask, "What is this story really about? What do I want my reader to know about me?" Then, they use all they know about narrative craft to bring that meaning forward.	Writers ask: • What is this story really about? • What do I want my reader to know about me? Then they use all they know about narrative craft to bring that meaning forward.
The writer is ready to use literary devices. This writer is successfully using a variety of narrative techniques and would benefit from learning to use literary devices. He has a clear sense of the meaning behind his story, as well as the places where this meaning might be emphasized or further revealed.	I think you are ready for a new challenge. When writers are strong—using all sorts of craft, writing focused, well-paced stories—it often signals that they are ready for something new. I've noticed that you are trying to bring out what your story is really about, and I want to teach you one way that writers do this: using literary devices. Writers use comparisons (like metaphors and similes), repetition, and even symbols to highlight important messages in stories.	Literary devices writers use to reveal meaning to a reader: • Metaphors and similes • Repetition • Symbolism
The writer summarizes rather than story-tells. There is probably a sense that this writer is disconnected from the series of events—listing what happened first, then next, then next. He writes predominately by overviewing what happened ("On the way to school I was almost attacked by a dog but I got there okay."). The writer rarely uses dialogue, descriptive details, or other forms of narrative craft to convey the story to his reader.	Writers don't take huge steps through their experience, writing like this: "I had an argument. Then I went to bed." Instead, writers take tiny steps, writing more like this: "'It was your turn!' I yelled, and then I turned and walked out of the room really fast. I slammed the door and went to my bedroom. I was so furious that I just sat on my bed for a long time." It helps to show what happened rather than just telling the main gist of it.	Not giant steps, but baby steps. Show, not tell.

If ...	After acknowledging what the child is doing well, you might say ...	Leave the writer with ...
Language		
The writer struggles with spelling. This writer's piece is riddled with spelling mistakes. This does not necessarily mean the writing is not strong (in fact, the story may be very strong), but the spelling mistakes compromise the reader's ability to understand it. The writer's struggle with spelling may stem from various places—difficulty understanding and applying spelling patterns, a limited stock of high-frequency words, lack of investment, the acquisition of English as a new language—and diagnosing the underlying problem will be an important precursor to teaching into it.	One of the things I'm noticing about your writing is how beautiful it sounds when you read it aloud. I looked more closely, curious about how I had missed all the beauty you've captured on this page, and realized that all your spelling mistakes make it difficult for me (and probably other readers, too) to understand. Today, I want to teach you a few techniques writers use to help them spell. Writers use the classroom word wall, they stretch words out and write down the sounds they hear, and they use words they *do* know how to spell to help them with those they don't know how to spell.	Writers work hard at their spelling. They: • Use the **word wall**. • **S-T-R-E-T-C-H** words out and write down the sounds they hear. • Use words they **know** (*found*), to help them spell words they **don't know** (*compound*, *round*).
The writer struggles with end punctuation. This story amounts to what appears to be one long, endless sentence. The writer may have distinct sentences ("We ran down the road James was chasing us we thought we needed to run faster to escape him") that are simply not punctuated. Alternatively, he may have strung his sentences together using an endless number of *and*s, *then*s, and *but*s in an attempt at cohesion. ("We ran down the road and James was chasing us and we thought that we needed to run faster to escape him but then we could hear his footsteps and his breathing and we were scared.")	I read your piece today, and it sounded a bit like this. "We ran down the road and James was chasing us and we thought that we needed to run faster to escape him but then we could hear his footsteps and his breathing and we were scared." Phew, I was out of breath! Today, I want to teach you that writers use end punctuation to give their readers a little break, to let them take a breath, before moving on to the next thing that happened in the story. One way to figure out where to put end punctuation is to reread your piece aloud, notice where you find yourself stopping to take a small breath, and put a period, exclamation point, or question mark there.	Writers reread their pieces aloud, notice where readers should stop and take a small breath because one thought has ended, and use end punctuation to help mark those places.
The Process of Generating Ideas		
The writer has "nothing to write about." This writer often leaves the minilesson, returns to his seat, and sits idly, waiting for you to visit. When you do visit, he is generally quick to tell you that he has "nothing to write about." This writer needs help with independence, but also with understanding that life is one big source of stories. As long as one is living, one has something to write about!	I'm noticing that you often have trouble finding things to write about, and I wanted to remind you that life is one big source of story ideas. Writers see the world through special eyes, imagining stories in the tiniest of moments. Writers find stories at the dinner table, while walking down the street, in the classroom, and at recess. Writers know that it matters less *what* they write about and more *how* they write about it.	Writers have the eyes to find stories everywhere. They know it matters less **what** they write about and more **how** they write about it.

If ...	After acknowledging what the child is doing well, you might say ...	Leave the writer with ...
The writer's notebook work does not represent all she can do. This writer is content to summarize and write in cursory ways in her notebook, and does not hold herself to using all she knows when collecting entries. This may mean the entries are short, underdeveloped, or lack narrative craft. When you look at this child's entries, you do not get the sense that she is striving to do her best work while collecting.	Many people think that the writer's notebook is just a place to collect stuff and that real writing happens when you pick a seed idea and draft on lined paper. I sort of get the idea you think that way. It is true that the notebook is a place for collecting, but it is also true that the notebook is a place for *practicing*. Today, I want to teach you that writers hold themselves accountable for using everything they know about good writing whenever they write, even in their notebooks. This includes everything they know about structure, storytelling, revision, and editing!	Writers use their notebooks to practice becoming better writers. They use everything they know about structure, storytelling, and even revision and editing!
The Process of Drafting		
The writer has trouble maintaining stamina and volume. This writer has a hard time putting words down on the page. It may be that he writes for a long period of time producing very little or that he refuses to write for longer than a few minutes. The writer often has avoidance behaviors (e.g., trips to the bathroom during writing workshop, a pencil tip that breaks repeatedly). He gets very little writing done during the workshop, despite urging from you.	Today, I want to teach you a little trick that often works for me when I'm having trouble staying focused. When writing is hard for me, I set small, manageable goals for myself. I make sure these goals are something I *know* I can do, like writing for ten minutes straight. Then, when I reach my goal, I give myself a little gift, like a short walk or a few minutes to sketch a picture. Then, I get back to writing again.	Writers set goals for themselves and work hard to achieve them. When they do, they reward themselves for their hard work.
The writer struggles to work independently. This student is often at your side, asking questions or needing advice. She struggles to write on her own and only seems to generate ideas when you are sitting beside her. When she does write, she needs constant "checks" and accolades. She is task-oriented. That is, she will complete one thing you have taught her to do and then sit and wait to be told what to do next. She does not rely on charts or other materials to keep her going.	As a writer, it is important that you take control of your own writing life. You can't be content to sit back and relax. Instead, you have to ask yourself, "What in this room might help me get back on track as a writer?" Then, you use those resources to get started again. You can look at charts in the room, ask your partner for help, read mentor texts for inspiration, or even look back over old writing for new ideas. or One thing I'm noticing about you as a writer is that you write with me in mind. What I mean by this is that when I teach something, you try it. When I suggest something, you try it. But I am not the only writing teacher in this room. Believe it or not, *you* can be your own writing teacher, too. Today, I want to teach you how to look at your own work against a checklist, assess for what is going well and what you might do better, and then set goals for how you might revise your current piece and for what you might try out in your future work, too.	When you are stuck, you can: • Consult charts • Ask your partner for help • Read mentor texts for inspiration • Look back over old writing for new ideas

If ...	After acknowledging what the child is doing well, you might say ...	Leave the writer with ...
The Process of Revision		
The writer does not seem to be driven by personal goals so much as by your instructions. If you ask, "What are you working on?" this writer acts surprised. "My writing," she says, and indeed, you are pretty sure that is what she is doing. She is trying to crank out the required amount of text. She doesn't have more specific goals about how to do things better that are influencing her.	Can I ask you something? Who is the boss of your writing? I'm asking that because you need to be the boss of your writing, and to be the best boss you can be, you need to give yourself little assignments. You need to take yourself by the hand and say, "From now on, you should be working on this," and then after a bit, "Now you should be working on this."	My Writing Goals Are: 1. _____ 2. _____ 3. _____
The Process of Editing		
The writer does not use what she knows about editing while writing. This writer is not applying what she knows about spelling, grammar, and punctuation while writing. You may notice that you have taught a particular spelling pattern, and she mastered it in isolation but is not using that knowledge during writing workshop. She may also spell word wall words incorrectly or misspell words that are similar (e.g., spelling *getting* correctly but misspelling *setting*). This writer needs to be reminded that editing is not something left for the last stages of writing. Instead, writers use all they know *as they write*.	You are the boss of your own writing, and part of being the boss is making sure that you are doing, and using, everything you know while you write. Often when people think of editing, they think of it as something they do just before publishing. This is true, but it is also true that writers edit as they write. Today, I want to teach you that writers use an editing checklist to remind them of what they've learned about spelling, punctuation, and grammar. They take a bit of time each day to make sure they are using all they know as they write.	Editing Checklist • Read, asking, "Will this make sense to a stranger?" • Check the punctuation. • Do your words look like they are spelled correctly?

Information Writing

If …	After acknowledging what the child is doing well, you might say …	Leave the writer with …
Structure and Cohesion		
The writer has not established a clear organizational structure. This writer is struggling with organization. It is likely that his book is a jumble of information about a larger topic, with no clear subheadings or internal organization. The writer may have a table of contents but the chapters actually contain a whole bunch of stuff unrelated to the chapter titles, or the writer may have skipped this part of the process altogether.	One of the most important things information writers do is organize their writing. Making chapters or headings is one way to make it easier for your readers to learn about your topic. It's like creating little signs that say, "Hey, reader, I'm about to start talking about a new part of my topic!" It helps to name what the upcoming part of your writing will be about and then to write about just that thing. When information writers notice they are about to start writing about something new, they often create a new heading that tells the reader what the next part will be about.	One thing ____ About that thing About that thing About that thing Another thing ____ About that next thing About that next thing ~~Something else~~ ~~Something else~~ Another thing ____ NOT: One thing Another thing The first thing A whole other thing
There is no logical order to the sequence of information. The writer has a clearly structured piece of writing and is ready to consider the logical order of the different sections of information. That is, she is ready to think about what sections of her text will come first, which will fall in the middle, and which will come last. In doing so, she will consider audience, as well as the strength of each part of her writing.	You are ready for a big new step. After writers learn to organize an information piece and have created perfectly structured sections and parts, they are often left asking, "What's next?" *What's next* is organizing again but doing it with more purpose. What I mean is this: writers ask, "Which part of my text should come first? Which should come second? What about third?" They think about what order makes the most sense for their particular topic. They might decide to organize from least to most important information, from weakest to strongest information, in chronological order, or in other ways.	Information writers sort their information **logically**. They might put the sections in order from least to most important, weakest to strongest, chronologically, or in other ways.

If ...	After acknowledging what the child is doing well, you might say ...	Leave the writer with ...
Information in various sections overlaps. This writer attempted to organize his piece, but has various sections that overlap. The writer may have repeated similar information in several parts of his piece or may have attempted to give the same information worded differently. Often he has sections and subsections that are too closely related and therefore struggles to find different information for different parts.	It is great that you have a system for organizing things. It is sort of like this page is a drawer and you just put things about (XYZ) in it. And this chapter is a drawer and you just put stuff about (ABC) in it. There are a few mess-ups—places where you have some whole other things scattered in, or some things that are in two places. That always happens. You've got to expect it. So what writers do is just what you have done. They write organized pieces. But then, when they are done writing, they ... Do you know? They reread to check. Just like you can reread to check your spelling, you can reread to check that the right things are in the right drawers, the right sections.	Writers reread to check that things are in the right drawers.
The writer is ready to experiment with alternative organizational structures. This writer may have a relatively strong organizational structure to her information piece, but you sense there are better options or more challenging avenues she might take. Then, too, she may have tried to organize her piece one way, but the topic does not lend itself well to the structure she has chosen. In either instance, she is ready to broaden her repertoire in regard to organizational structure and study mentor texts to imagine alternate ways her text might go.	One of the greatest things about information writing is that there are so many different ways a text can go. If we were to lay out a few different books on the same topic, we would find dozens of different ways the authors chose to organize them. Some authors, like Gail Gibbons, write chronologically, others write about different sections of a topic, and some authors use pros and cons or questions and answers to organize their information. The options are endless! When writers are looking to challenge themselves and try out some new ways of organizing their writing, they study mentor texts. One way to study an information text is to read, asking, "How does this author structure and organize his information?" Then, you can try out the same structure with your own writing.	Information writers study mentor texts and ask, "How does this author structure and organize his information? Then, they try the same with their own writing.
The writer has chosen a topic that is too broad. This writer has chosen a topic that is broad, such as dogs or the Civil War, and has likely created a table of contents that suggests the product will be more of an all-about book. In an attempt to make his writing more sophisticated, and the process of crafting an information piece more demanding, you will want to teach him to narrow his topic a bit.	I was looking at your topic choice earlier and thought to myself, "He is ready for a challenge!" You chose a topic that is very broad, very big. There is nothing wrong with that. In fact, it means you'll have a lot to say! But when information writers want to push themselves, when they want to craft a text that is more sophisticated, they narrow their topic. Today, I'm going to teach you how to narrow your topic by asking, "What is *one part* of this subject I can write a lot about?"	Writers challenge themselves by narrowing their topics. They ask, "What is *one part* of this subject I can write a lot about?"

If …	After acknowledging what the child is doing well, you might say …	Leave the writer with …
The piece lacks an introduction and/or a conclusion. This writer has written an information piece that is missing an introduction and/or conclusion. Alternatively, it may be that the writer attempted to introduce and then conclude her piece but did so in overly folksy or ineffective ways. (For instance, she might have begun, "My name is Michelle, and I'm going to teach you everything you want to know about sharks. They are really cool." Later, she'll likely end along the same lines: "That's everything about sharks! I hope you learned a lot!") She is ready to adopt a more sophisticated tone and learn more nuanced (and subtle) ways of pulling readers in and providing closure.	In stories, writers use introductions to pull their readers in. Their conclusions, or endings, usually give the reader some closure. Really, information writing isn't much different. Writers use introductions to *pull* readers in, often by giving them a little information on the topic (orienting them). Then, they give their reader a sense of closure by wrapping things up with a conclusion (sometimes restating some key points about the topic) and leaving the reader with something to think about.	Introductions pull readers in: • Give a bit of information about the topic. Orient your reader. Conclusions give readers closure and wrap things up: • Restate a bit about the topic. • Leave your reader with something to think about.
Elaboration		
Each section is short and needs elaboration. This writer has attempted to group her information, but each section is short. For example, she may have listed one or two facts related to a specific subsection but is stuck for what to add next.	Information writers need to be able to say a lot about each part of their topic, or to elaborate. There are a few things you can do to make each part of your book chock-full of information. One thing that helps is to write in partner sentences. This means that instead of writing one sentence about each thing, you can push yourself to write two sentences (or more) about each thing. So if I said, "George sits at a desk when he is at school" and I wanted to write with partner sentences, what else might I say about George sitting at his desk?" You are right. It can help to fill in stuff about why, kinds of, where, how many, and so on. A whole other thing you can do to get yourself to say more is to use prompts like, "It's also important to know this because …"; "Also …"; and "What this means is …"	Writers Elaborate 1. They check to make sure they have at least four or five pieces of information for each subtopic. If not, they consider cutting that section and starting a new one. 2. Writers elaborate by creating partner sentences. 3. They use prompts like "It's also important to know …"; "Also …"; and "What this means is …" to say more about a particular piece of information.

If ...	After acknowledging what the child is doing well, you might say ...	Leave the writer with ...
The writer elaborates by adding fact upon fact. This writer has elaborated but has done so by adding fact upon fact upon fact. As a result, his writing reads like a list rather than a cohesive section of text. This writer would benefit from learning to add a bit of his own voice back into his writing, relying not just on factual information, but on his own ability to synthesize and make sense of these facts for the reader.	You have tackled the first step in information writing—gathering the information needed to support various subtopics. Here's the thing, though. Writers don't *just* list facts for readers. It is also their job to take these facts and make something of them, to help explain why they are important to the reader. Writers often use prompts like "In other words ... ," "What this really means is ... ," "This shows ... ," and "All of this is important because ..." to help readers understand the information they've put forth.	Information writers don't just list fact after fact. They *spice up* their writing by adding a bit of their own voice: • "In other words ..." • "What this really means is ..." • "This shows ..." • "All of this is important because ..."
The writer goes off on tangents when elaborating. This writer has tried to elaborate on information but tends to get into personal and tangential details ("Dogs really are great pets. I have a dog, too. I had a cat, too, but she peed on the counter so my Dad got rid of her.") Or by repeating the same information again and again. Or by being chit-chatty ("And I love LOVE that and think it is really funny, so so funny.")	You are working hard to say a lot about your topic, aren't you? I have to give you a tip, though. Sometimes, in your hard work to say a lot, you are doing things that don't really work that well. Let me give you an example of things that don't work when writers are writing information books, and will you see if you do those things some of the time? Pretend I was writing about dogs, so I wrote that there are many kinds of dogs, and the kinds of dogs are divided into groups, like spaniels, retrievers, toy dogs, and so forth. If I then said, "And I have a dog and a cat, too, and the cat's name is Barney ..." would that go in my report? You are right. It wouldn't go because it isn't really teaching information and ideas about the topic—and it might not even be about the topic. If I wrote "And I Love Love LOVE dogs," would that go? And if I said, "Some dogs are spaniels, some are retrievers," would that go? You see, there are things people do when they are trying to elaborate, to say more, that just don't work that well. So what writers do is they cross them out and try other ways to elaborate. You will want to reread your writing and to have the courage to say no sometimes. or Today, I want to teach you that information writers revise by checking to make sure all their information is important and new. They cut out parts where they started to talk about their own life too much and got off topic, parts where they included information that doesn't go with what they were writing about, or parts where they repeat the same thing more than once.	Information writers cut parts where: • They started talking about their life too much and got off topic. • They included information that doesn't fit with what the rest of the paragraph is about. • They repeated something they'd already written.

If ...	After acknowledging what the child is doing well, you might say ...	Leave the writer with ...
The writer does not elaborate on information from outside sources. The writer has included information from outside sources, such as quotes, facts, or statistics, but does not elaborate on this information for his reader. As a result, his writing is often very short and hops from interesting fact to interesting fact.	I love all the research you have included in your information piece. It really shows that you are an expert on this topic. One way to show you are an expert, to show all you know about your topic, is by including outside information like quotes, facts, and statistics. Another way to be an expert and teach your readers (the way I'm going to teach you today) is by elaborating on those facts. Today, I want to teach you that writers don't just plop information into their writing. Instead, they explain what it means to their readers by using phrases like "What this means is ..." or "In other words ..."	Writers don't just plop information into their writing. Instead, they explain what it means to their readers by using phrases like "What this means is ..." or "In other words ..."
Language		
The writer incorporates quotes, facts, and statistics but does so awkwardly. This writer uses quotes, facts, statistics, and other outside information to elaborate on the sections of his information text. The information is well organized, and the facts and quotes are generally well placed but often sound awkward. It is not clear that the writer understands how to move from his words to the words and examples of an author or experts, and he needs help with ways to do this more fluently.	Quotes, facts, and statistics are incredibly important in information writing because they tell a reader that, yes, I have done my research and know a lot about my topic! Today, I want to teach you how to take quotes, facts, and statistics and make them sound like a part of your writing. You can do this by using transitional phrases like *for instance*, *one example*, or *according to*.	Writers use transitional phrases to introduce quotes, facts, and statistics. Example: Sharks aren't that dangerous. One example of this is basking sharks. People in the Hamptons often see them and they are slow-moving and harmless. According to Science-Facts.com, "more people die of alligator attacks than shark attacks."
Transitions from section to section sound awkward. This writer has organized her information piece into sections and paragraphs, but the transitions from part to part feel awkward. She would benefit from a few tips aimed at helping her ease readers into each new section of her text.	One of the hardest parts about being an information writer is moving from one part of a topic to the next. One second a writer is talking about the Lewis and Clark expedition, and the next second she is talking about the Louisiana Purchase. In her mind she knows how these two things connect (they are both about the Westward Expansion), but this isn't always clear to her readers. Today, I want to teach you how to write a topic sentence that reminds readers what your big topic is and introduces them to what your next section will be about. One way writers do this is by connecting each section back to the larger topic.	Information writers use topic sentences to say what a section will be about and explain how it relates to the big, overall topic. Example: Lewis and Clark were famous explorers who took on a daring adventure. They were an important part of the Westward Expansion. or Another important part of the Westward Expansion was the Louisiana Purchase, because it gave Americans new land to explore and settle.

If ...	After acknowledging what the child is doing well, you might say ...	Leave the writer with ...
The writer does not incorporate domain-specific vocabulary. This writer has written about a topic but has done so without incorporating domain-specific vocabulary. It may be that the child simply glossed over using terms such as *caravan* or *brigade* (because he did not understand them or know how to incorporate them into his own writing) or used simpler language in place of complex vocabulary.	As an information writer, it's important that you come across as an expert on your topic. Readers expect to learn something new, and one way to teach them something new is by using technical, expert vocabulary. Today, I want to teach you that writers don't just toss these words into their writing, though. Instead, they learn what they mean, and then they define them for their readers. They can either say the word and then its definition, or tuck the word's definition into a sentence using commas.	Information writers use expert vocabulary (and define it for their readers, too). They can: • Say the word and then explain what it means. Example: Loyalists were people who remained loyal to the king during the American Revolution. • Tuck the definition into the sentence using two commas. Example: Loyalists, people who remained loyal to the king during the American Revolution, fought throughout the war.
The Process of Generating Ideas		
The writer chooses topics about which she has little expertise and/or that are difficult to research. This child often generates ideas quickly, and they often relate to her passions. She might decide to write about the melting of the polar ice caps and its effect on seals during a unit in which students are writing about areas of personal expertise or access to research material on that topic is limited and difficult to comprehend. This child needs help mining her life for topics that are closer to home and assessing her own ability to write long, strong, and focused about a particular topic.	Writers ask themselves some tough questions when they are choosing a topic for information writing. They ask: 1. Do I care about this topic? (You are already doing this!) 2. Do I know enough to imagine a possible table of contents? 3. Do I know one or two resources I can use to gather more information? If not, they pick a different topic.	When Choosing a Topic, Information Writers Ask: • Do I care about this topic? • Do I know enough to imagine a possible table of contents? • Do I know one or two resources I can use to gather more information?
The writer simply copies facts into his notebook. This writer's "collecting" amounts to copying facts from books into his notebook. He copies lines verbatim, rarely bothering to paraphrase or quote. It may seem as if the child is not being overly discriminatory about what to include. That is, if the book says it, he writes it. In this way, the child's notebook becomes an endless list of facts about a topic or, if the child has created organized categories, parts of a topic.	Research is a pretty hard thing to do as a writer. Researchers have a difficult job: They have to take the information that other people have written, sort through it, and then put it into their own words or quote it. You can't just copy what other authors have written into your notebook, because that would be stealing their words! Today, I want to teach you one way that writers take information from a book and incorporate it into their own writing. It's called paraphrasing. To paraphrase (or put something into your own words), it helps to read a chunk of text, close the book, say back an important part of what you just read, and then put it into your own words.	One way researchers put information into their own words is by paraphrasing. They: 1. Read a chunk of the text. 2. Close the book. 3. Say back an important part of what they just read. 4. Put it into their own words.

If ...	After acknowledging what the child is doing well, you might say ...	Leave the writer with ...
The Process of Drafting		
The first draft is not organized. This writer has written a first draft that is disorganized. It may be that there is an underlying organizational structure (e.g., the writer grouped similar information together), but she did not use new pages, section titles, or transitions to let the reader in on this structure. Alternatively, the writer may have simply "written a draft," compiling all the information she collected into one ongoing piece of writing.	One of the most important things information writers do is organize. It can be hard for a reader to learn a lot of new information about, say, sharks. But when a writer organizes the information into sections, then it becomes easier for the reader to take it in. The reader knows that one part will be about sharks' bodies, another will be about what they eat, and another will be about their family life. As a writer, it's important to look at your draft and make sure that you've organized it in a way that will make sense to the reader. This usually means taking all the information or facts about one part of a topic (like sharks' bodies) and putting that together. Then, taking all the information about another topic (like what sharks eat) and putting that together. Then using section headings to make it clear what each part is about.	Information Writers Organize Their Writing! • Divide your topic into sections (you may have already done this while planning). • Put the information about one section together with a heading. • Put the information about another section together with a heading. • And so on ... (Sometimes it helps to cut up your draft and tape different parts together!)
The Process of Revision		
The writer is "done" before revising. This writer is perfectly pleased with his first draft and declares, "I'm done" soon after completing it. Your revision minilessons do little to help inspire this writer to revise, and you feel you must constantly sit by his side and point out parts to revise in order for him to do the work.	I've noticed that you often have trouble thinking of ways to revise your piece. You write a draft and then it feels done. Sometimes when it is hard to come up with ideas for improving your writing, it helps to have a published writer help. You just look at a published book that you love and notice cool things that the author has done, then you revise to do those same things in your writing.	When writers feel done, they study a few mentor texts asking, "What has this writer done that I could try as well?"
The writer does not have a large repertoire of strategies to draw from. This writer lives off of each day's minilesson. She is task-oriented and generally applies (or attempts to apply) what you teach each day. This student is living on your day-to-day teaching as if it is all she has, rather than drawing on a large repertoire of known writing techniques and strategies.	Whenever I teach something, I love to see kids like you go off and give it a go. It means they are pushing themselves to try new things. But I also hope that isn't *all* kids do. We've talked about how writers carry invisible backpacks full of strategies. When I teach a minilesson, I give you something new to add to your backpack, but it is important to use everything else you have in there, too! Today, I want to teach you one way writers remind themselves of what they already know about revision. They look at artifacts like classroom charts and our information writing checklist and look back at old entries to remind themselves of the strategies they know. Then, they write an action plan.	Take Action! 1. Look at charts, your notebook, and the Information Writing Checklist. 2. Make a list of the ways you could revise. 3. Create an action plan for yourself.

If ...	After acknowledging what the child is doing well, you might say ...	Leave the writer with ...
The Process of Editing		
The writer has edited but has missed several mistakes or would otherwise benefit from learning to partner-edit. This writer often thinks she has written what she intended to say, and therefore she overlooks many mistakes. She would benefit from learning to edit with a partner before publishing her writing.	I know that you have worked hard to use many of the editing strategies you know and have made many changes to your piece. As a result, it is clearer and more readable. Sometimes as a writer, though, you know so clearly what you *wanted* to say that you miss places where you may have said something in a confusing or incorrect way. That's why most writers have editors that look at their writing once it's done. Today, I want to teach you a few things you and your writing partner can do together. You can: • Read your piece aloud and ask your partner to check to make sure what you say matches what he or she sees. • Circle words you think are misspelled and try to figure them out together. • Use the class editing checklist together.	A Few Things You and Your Writing Partner Might Say to Each Other • "Reread your piece, and I'll make sure what you say matches what I see." • "Let's circle the words that we think are misspelled and try them again." • "Let's use our class editing checklist to proofread your piece."

Opinion Writing

If ...	After acknowledging what the child is doing well, you might say ...	Leave the writer with ...
Structure and Cohesion		
The introduction does not forecast the structure of the essay. The writer has made a claim and supported it with reasons, but there is no forecasting statement early on in the essay that foreshadows the reasons to come. Instead, it seems as if the writer thought of and wrote about one reason, then, when reaching the end of that first body paragraph, thought, "What's another reason?" and then raised and elaborated upon that reason. He is ready to learn to plan for the overarching structure of his argument and forecast that structure in the introduction.	You have definitely learned to make a claim in your essay and to support that claim with reasons. There is one big step you need to take, though, and that is to let your reader know how your essay will go from the very beginning, in the introduction. Today, I want to teach you that opinion writers forecast how their writing will go. They do this by stating their claim in the introduction and then adding on, "I think this because ..." Then they list the reasons that they will write about in the body of their piece.	Writers use the introduction to forecast how their opinion pieces will go. 1. State your claim. • "I think ..." 2. Tell your reader why your claim is true. • "One reason I think ... is because ..." • "Another reason I think ... is because ..." • "The final reason I think ... is because ..."
Supports overlap. In this instance, the writer has developed supporting reasons that are overlapping or overly similar. While this may pose few problems now, the writer will struggle when the time comes to find examples to support each reason (because the examples will be the same!). For example, if a student argues, "Dogs make the best pets," she may provide the following reasons: they like to play games, they cheer you up, and they are great at playing fetch. Playing fetch and playing games overlap, and you'll want to help this student find another, different, reason why dogs are great pets.	Sometimes, when writers develop supporting reasons for their thesis, they find that one or more of them overlap. What I mean by this is that they basically say the same thing! Today, I want to teach you that writers look at their supporting reasons with a critical eye, checking to see if any overlap. One way they do this is by listing the examples they'll use for each paragraph. If some of the examples are the same, then the reasons are probably too similar!	Are your supporting reasons too similar? Test them to find out! Support _____ Example #1: Example #2: Support _____ Example #1: Example #2: Support _____ Example #1: Example #2:

If …	After acknowledging what the child is doing well, you might say …	Leave the writer with …
Supports are not parallel or equal in weight. This writer has developed a thesis and supports. While all the supports may support the writer's overall claim, they are not parallel. For instance, when arguing that "dogs make great friends," the writer may have suggested that this is because (A) they always listen to you, (B) they play with you, and (C) one time I was sad and my dog cuddled with me. Supports A and B are both reasons or ways that dogs can make great friends. Support C is an example of *one time* a dog made a good friend. This writer needs help identifying places where one or more supports are not parallel and/or are not equal in weight to the others.	As a writer, you want each part of your essay to be about equal in weight. What I mean by this is that all your supports should prove your overall claim *and* they should be something you can elaborate on with several examples. Today, I want to teach you that writers look back over their supports and ask, "Are these all equal in size?" One way they test out this question is by checking to see if they can give two to three examples for each support. If they can't, they have to revise the supporting reason to make it bigger.	Do you have examples to prove each of your supports? Support _____ Example #1: Example #2: Support _____ Example #1: Example #2: Support _____ Example #1: Example #2:
The writer is new to the writing workshop or this particular genre of writing. This writer struggles not because she has struggled to raise the level of her opinion writing, but because this is a new genre for her. She may display certain skill sets (e.g., the ability to elaborate or write with beautiful descriptions) but lacks the vision of what she is being asked to produce. Her piece may be unfocused or disorganized. It also may be sparse, lacking any sort of elaboration.	As a writer, it can be particularly hard to write well if you don't have a vision, a mental picture, of what you hope to produce. Today, I want to teach you that one way writers learn about the kinds of writing they hope to produce is by studying mentor texts. They read a mentor text once, enjoying it as a piece of writing. Then, they read it again, this time asking, "How do opinion pieces seem to go?" They label what they notice and then try it in their own writing.	Writers use mentor texts to help them imagine what they hope to write. They: 1. Read the text and enjoy it as a piece of writing. 2. Ask, "How do opinion pieces seem to go?" 3. Label what they notice. 4. Try some of what they noticed in their own writing.
The writer has a number of well-developed reasons, but they blur together without paragraphs or transitions. This writer has developed multiple reasons to support his opinion and has supported those reasons with evidence. It is difficult to discern an organizational structure in the piece, however, because many of the reasons blur together without paragraphs or transitions.	A paragraph is like a signal to a reader. It says, "I just made an important point. Now I'm moving on to something else." Paragraphs give readers an opportunity to take in evidence part by part, reason by reason. Readers expect that opinion writers will separate their reasons in paragraphs, with one section for each reason. Writers reread their writing, take note of when they've moved from one reason to another, and insert a paragraph there.	Opinion writers use paragraphs to separate their reasons. Each paragraph has: Reasons + Evidence

If ...	After acknowledging what the child is doing well, you might say ...	Leave the writer with ...
The writer is ready to consider counterarguments. This writer has shown evidence that she is ready to consider counterarguments. She may have written something like, "I know that not everyone agrees, but …" or may have gone further and laid out the opposing argument that others might make. She is ready to learn to use counterarguments to bolster her own argument.	You are doing one of the hardest things there is to do when you are working to write an argument. You are imagining the people who might disagree with you and trying to see an opposite point of view from your own. Today, I want to show you how to raise the level of that work by teaching you to use counterarguments to *make your own argument stronger*! One way to do this is by showing that there are flaws or gaps or problems in the counterargument, and then show how *your* argument addresses those problems. So you might start by saying, "This argument overlooks …" or "This argument isn't showing the full story."	Strong opinion writers expose the flaws, gaps, and problems in counterarguments and then show how their argument addresses those problems. They might begin: • "This argument overlooks …" • "This argument isn't showing the full story."
Elaboration		
The writer is struggling to elaborate (1). This writer has an opinion, as well as several reasons to support that opinion, but most reasons are stated without elaboration. He may have created a long list of reasons to support his opinion, but does not say more about any one reason or provide examples or evidence to support his reasons.	You know that when you give an opinion, you need to support it with reasons! But opinion writers don't just stop with reasons. Today, I want to teach you that when writers come up with a reason to support a claim, they then try to write a whole paragraph about that reason. One way to do this is by shifting into a mini-story. You can start your claim and reason and then write, "For example, one day …" or "For example, in the text …" and tell a mini-story that shows and proves your reason.	One way writers elaborate on a reason is by providing a mini-story to prove their point. They might write: • "For example, one day …" (personal essay) or • "For example, in the text …" (literary or argument essay)
The writer is struggling to elaborate (2). This writer has an opinion, as well as several reasons to support that opinion, but most reasons are stated without elaboration. She may have created an endless list of reasons to support her opinion, but does not say more about any one reason or provide examples and evidence to support it. She has learned to use mini-stories to support her reasons and is ready for a larger repertoire of evidence.	You know that when you give an opinion, you need to support it with reasons! But opinion writers don't just stop with reasons. They need evidence to convince their readers that their claim is right. Today, I want to teach you that when writers come up with reasons to support a claim, they then try to write a whole paragraph about that reason. One way to do this is by adding facts, statistics, definitions, and quotes that support your reason. Writers have to choose the evidence that makes the most sense for them.	Opinion writers support reasons using: • Mini-stories • Facts • Statistics • Definitions • Quotes
The writer's evidence feels free-floating or disconnected from the argument at hand. This writer has elaborated on reasons using evidence but has done little to explain that evidence to his reader. He'll often drop a fact or statistic into a paragraph and may even recognize that it feels awkward. He needs strategies for elaborating on evidence, specifically by learning to tie it back to the overarching claim.	You have elaborated by providing not only reasons to support your claim, but evidence as well. Sometimes, when writers write persuasively, they incorporate facts and statistics and mini-stories, only to find that these feel awkward or disconnected from their own writing. Writers have a trick to fix this problem, and that is what I want to teach you today! One way writers make evidence particularly persuasive is by saying a bit about how that evidence relates to their claim. They might say, "This proves …" or "This shows that _____ is true because …"	Writers don't just toss evidence into an opinion piece. Instead, they help their readers understand why it is there! They can help explain the importance of the evidence by writing things like: • "This proves …" • "This shows that ____ is true because …"

If ...	After acknowledging what the child is doing well, you might say ...	Leave the writer with ...
The piece is swamped with details. This writer is attempting to be convincing and knows that details matter. His writing is riddled with facts, details, quotes, and other forms of evidence in support of his thesis. Because the writing is so detail-heavy, the writer has likely struggled to fully integrate the evidence or explain it to his reader.	You are the kind of writer who knows that details matter. Today, I want to teach you that choosing the just-right details and cutting others can make your piece even better. One way to know what details to keep and what details to cut is to read each piece of evidence and ask, "Is that evidence the *most* convincing evidence I can give to convince my readers of my opinion?" Then you make some hard choices—keeping the best evidence and cutting the rest.	Opinion writers choose evidence carefully and critically! • Look at each piece of evidence and ask, "Is that evidence the *most* convincing evidence I can give?" • Then, keep the best evidence and cut the rest.
The writer has provided evidence, but it does not all support the claim. This writer has elaborated on her reasons with a variety of evidence, but not all of this evidence matches the point she is trying to make. It may be that a mini-story is unfocused and not angled to support a particular point. It may be that a quote or statistic does not connect directly to the claim. Either way, this writer needs help rereading her piece with a critical lens, checking to be sure that each sentence she has written helps to further her opinion.	As a writer, you know it is important not just to give a bunch of reasons for a claim, but also to spend time *proving* those reasons. You have already done this by including all sorts of evidence. Today I want to teach you that after collecting evidence, writers go back to look at their writing with a critical lens. They ask, "Does this piece of evidence match my reason? Does it really prove what I am trying to say?" If it matches, they keep it. If not, they cut it out.	Opinion writers ask: • Does this piece of evidence match my reason? • Does this prove what I am trying to say? If so, they keep it! If not, they cut it!

Language		
The writer uses a casual, informal tone when writing. As you read this writer's opinion pieces, you are overwhelmed by a sense of casualness and informality. Likely this comes from a good place on the writer's part. He may be trying to communicate directly with his audience. ("Hey, wait, stop and think before you throw that piece of garbage on the ground.") He may also be attempting to be convincing. ("Littering is SOOOO bad for the environment and kills animals every day!!") There is nothing wrong with this, but you sense that this writer is ready to move toward more sophisticated forms of persuasion, beginning with the adoption of a more formal, academic tone.	As an opinion writer, your first and foremost job is to convince readers that your claim, your opinion, is correct. When you first start out as a persuasive writer, you learn fun little ways to do this, like talking to the reader or making exaggerations. But as you grow as a writer, the challenge becomes, "How do I make my writing equally as persuasive but do it in a way that sounds more sophisticated, more professional, more grown up?" Today, I want to teach you a few tricks for adopting a more formal tone in your writing. When writers want to sound more formal they: • Use expert vocabulary • Use sophisticated transition words and phrases • Incorporate startling facts from credible sources	Sound like an expert! • Use expert vocabulary related to your topic. Example: When talking about the environment you might use words like, *biodegradable* or *ozone* • Use sophisticated transition words to introduce insights, ideas, or examples. Examples: *alternately*, *additionally*, *furthermore* • Incorporate startling facts from credible sources. Example: "You may not have known that, according to recycling-revolution.com, recycling one aluminum can saves enough energy to power a TV for three hours!

If …	After acknowledging what the child is doing well, you might say …	Leave the writer with …
The writer struggles with spelling. This writer's piece is riddled with spelling mistakes. This does not necessarily mean the writing is not strong (in fact, the essay he wrote may be very strong), but the spelling mistakes compromise the reader's ability to understand it. The writer's struggle with spelling may stem from various causes—difficulty with understanding and applying spelling patterns, a limited stock of high-frequency words, lack of investment, the acquisition of English as a new language—and diagnosing the underlying problem will be an important precursor to teaching into it.	When an opinion piece (or any piece of writing, really) is full of spelling mistakes, it can be hard for readers to understand what you are trying to say. Today, I want to remind you that writers try out multiple ways to spell a word before settling on one. Then, if they are still stuck, they consult a friend, writing partner, word wall, or other classroom resource.	Writers work hard at their spelling. They: 1. Try multiple versions of a word in the margin. 2. Pick the one that looks right. 3. Consult a peer, word wall, or other resource to help.
The writer struggles with comma usage. This writer is attempting to form more complex sentences but is struggling with the process. It may be that she uses commas incorrectly, interspersing them throughout the piece with little rhyme or reason, or that she simply doesn't use commas at all, resulting in long, difficult-to-read sentences. Either way, this writer needs help understanding the ways commas are used in sentences.	I've noticed that you've been trying to write longer, more complex sentences. Because of this, your writing sounds more like talking. It is quite beautiful. When writers write sentences that are more complex, though, they often need to use commas. Commas help readers know where to pause and help the sentence make sense. Today, I want to teach you a few important ways that writers use commas. Writers use commas in lists, to separate two or more adjectives, before (and sometimes after) names of people, and to separate two strong clauses that are also separated by a conjunction.	Use Commas To separate items in a list: • I want pears, apples and oranges. To separate adjectives: • He drove by in his red, shiny car. Before and after names of people: • My brother, Peter, is a good friend. • John, don't be so silly! To separate two strong clauses that are separated by a conjunction: • I am working hard, but she is resting on the couch. • She is taking an afternoon nap, and then we will go out for dinner.

If ...	After acknowledging what the child is doing well, you might say ...	Leave the writer with ...
The Process of Generating Ideas		
The writer struggles to generate meaningful topics worth exploring. This writer feels stuck and has difficulty generating ideas for writing. Sometimes this manifests through avoidance behaviors (going to the bathroom, sharpening pencils), and other times the child simply seems to be in a constant state of "thinking," not writing. This child needs help not only with generating ideas, but also with learning to independently use a repertoire of strategies when stuck.	I've noticed that coming up with ideas has been hard for you and that you've had to spend a lot of time thinking about what to write. When you write opinion pieces, you want them to be persuasive. And for them to be persuasive, you have to *care* a lot about the topic! It can help to think about what you really care the most about—think about things you love or hate ... and then see if you can write opinion pieces about that.	Write what you love, write what you hate. Not in between.
The writer is exploring opinions that are overly simple or without dimension. This writer's notebook is full of entries about topics that are safe and relatively one-sided. If writing about his own life, he may be writing about how he loves his brother or how candy is the best treat. When writing about texts, the writer is apt to pick simple, obvious points to argue. Based on the work you see this child doing on a regular basis, you are sure that he is capable of developing more complex theses—those that take into account various points of view or that argue claims that are more difficult to prove.	You have been writing about clear, concise opinions like "Dogs make the best pets" and "My mom is my best friend." Today, I want to show you how to raise the level of the thinking work you are doing by raising the level of your thesis. One way to do this is by picking an issue that people have different opinions on. You can write first to explore one side of the argument, and then write to explore the other side.	Writers make their ideas more complex by exploring issues with multiple sides. "On the one hand, people think ..." "On the other hand, people think ..."
The Process of Drafting		
The writer has a clear plan for her writing but loses focus and organization when drafting. This writer seemed to have a clear structural plan for her writing. She went into the process with folders full of evidence or neatly sorted booklets. But, as she began drafting, all this organization seemed to fly out the window. That is to say, this writer put pen to paper and wrote, wrote, wrote—leaving behind any thoughts of groupings and paragraphs.	As opinion writers, it is important to make an argument in a clear, organized way. This allows the reader to follow what you are saying point by point. To create an organized argument, opinion writers make sure they rely on the plans they've created. It often helps to draft each part of your essay on a separate piece of paper, dedicating a new sheet to each reason. Then, when you are finished, you paste it all together.	Writers Don't Leave Their Plans Behind! One way to make sure your drafts stay organized is to draft each section of your essay on a separate sheet of paper. Use a new sheet for each reason, and then paste the pages together at the end.

If …	After acknowledging what the child is doing well, you might say …	Leave the writer with …
The Process of Revision		
The writer has a limited repertoire of revision strategies. This writer lives off of each day's minilesson. He is task-oriented and generally applies (or attempts to apply) what you teach each day. This writer may work hard to revise, but when asked what else he might work on, he struggles to answer the question. This student is living on your day-to-day teaching as if it is all he has, rather than drawing on a large repertoire of known writing techniques and strategies.	As a writer, it is important that you take control of your own writing life. Writers use all they know about revision to make their pieces stronger. One way writers push themselves to get even stronger at writing is by studying mentor texts. They look at texts that resemble the kind they hope to create, find places that seem powerful and convincing, and then ask themselves, "What has the writer done to make these parts so powerful and convincing?" Then they try out the same in their own writing.	Writers study mentor authors to help them revise. They: 1. Study a piece that resembles the kind they hope to create. 2. Find places that seem powerful and convincing. 3. Ask, "What has the writer done to make these parts so powerful and convincing?" 4. Try the same in their own writing.
The Process of Editing		
The writer edits "on the run," investing little time or effort in the process. This writer is not applying what she knows about spelling, grammar, and punctuation while writing. It may be that you have taught a particular spelling pattern, and she mastered it in isolation but is not using that knowledge during writing workshop. She may also spell word wall words incorrectly or other words that are known (or easily referenced). There is often a sense that the writer does not care about the editing process, viewing it as a cursory last step before publication.	One thing I'm noticing is that editing goes awfully quickly for you and that many times you skip over mistakes. I've even seen you misspell a few words that are right up here on our word wall! Today, I want to teach you that editing is a multistep process and something that writers have to take seriously. One way to focus all your attention on editing is to pick one lens first—let's say ending punctuation—and read through your piece looking *only* for places where you need to add ending punctuation. Then you pick a second thing to look for, like checking to make sure your use of *to*, *two*, and *too* is correct. And again, you read through looking for only those mistakes. Writers do this until they've made it through the entire editing checklist.	Writers take each item on the editing checklist *one by one*. Editing checklist: • Read, asking, "Will this make sense to a stranger?" • Check the punctuation. • Do your words look like they are spelled correctly?